THE 10 BEST
ANXIETY
BUSTERS

THE 10 BEST ANXIETY BUSTERS

SIMPLE STRATEGIES TO TAKE CONTROL OF YOUR WORRY

DR. MARGARET WEHRENBERG

W. W. NORTON & COMPANY

NEW YORK • LONDON

For information about permission to reproduce selections from this book, write to Permissions, W. W. Norton & Company, Inc., 500 Fifth Avenue, New York, NY 10110

For information about special discounts for bulk purchases, please contact W. W. Norton Special Sales at specialsales@wwnorton.com or 800-233-4830

Manufacturing by RR Donnelley, Harrisonburg, VA
Book design by Molly Heron
Production manager: Leeann Graham

Library of Congress Cataloging-in-Publication Data

Wehrenberg, Margaret.
The 10 best anxiety busters : simple strategies to take control of your worry / Dr. Margaret Wehrenberg. — First Edition.
pages cm
Includes bibliographical references and index.
ISBN 978-0-393-71076-2 (pbk.)
1. Anxiety. I. Title. II. Title: Ten best anxiety busters.
BF575.A6W43994 2015
152.4′6—dc23

2014027706

W. W. Norton & Company, Inc., 500 Fifth Avenue, New York, N. Y. 10110
www.wwnorton.com
W. W. Norton & Company Ltd., Castle House, 75/76 Wells Street, London W1T 3QT

1 2 3 4 5 6 7 8 9 0

To my personal Anxiety Busters:
you know who you are—
you are on my speed dial!

CONTENTS

Contents

ACKNOWLEDGMENTS

FIRST AND FOREMOST, I want to acknowledge my editors. Andrea Dawson is such an inspiration and supporter. She always has a new idea and helps me execute it. She is also one of the kindest people I know and has such good sense about what will work in my books. That means she can steer me in the right direction without hurting my feelings.

Casey Ruble is a wonder. She can take whatever I have written and improve on it. She always makes sure my ideas are clear. The wonder of it is that she can do this and make it sound like my voice, only better.

I try not to burden my friends too much with hearing about the book while it is in progress, but I must say that everyone should be so blessed with such encouraging people in their lives. All in their own way have made this book come to fruition: Shannon and Susan, Mike, MJ, Cathy, the Pittsburgh

Three, Lurlene and MaryLou, Ellie and Hal, and my eight brothers and sisters and their spouses and children.

Those who have offered me speaking engagements have been surprisingly helpful because the opportunities to share what I am doing connect me with the very consumers and professionals who are asking important questions. There is nothing like being asked a tough question to push a person to learn more, if only to be able to answer it in the future. I can only hope these opportunities to share and learn continue.

I also want to acknowledge the grace of my clients. I am humbled by their trust and hope in the face of the pain they experience. Every day they make me want to know more so that I can help each one of them recover more quickly.

THE 10 BEST
ANXIETY
BUSTERS

A Worried Mind, and Body Too: What Kind of Anxiety Do *You* Have?

HAVE YOU EVER suddenly felt like your throat was closing up and you couldn't catch your breath? Like your chest was tightening, and you were getting dizzy, and you might pass out or even die? Maybe it happened before you boarded an airplane, or as you entered a crowded restaurant. Maybe it just happened out of the blue, with no apparent reason at all.

Or have you ever sat in a business meeting, or arrived at a party, and suddenly felt exposed—like all eyes were on you, but not in a good way? Did you blush, start to sweat, feel your hands tremble, or worry that you'd say something stupid? Did you find yourself avoiding similar situations after that?

Or how about those more vague but stubbornly persistent feelings of worry that just won't go away? That lump in your stomach that keeps telling you something's wrong—very wrong—even when you logically know there's nothing to fret about?

If you've had any of these experiences, you may be suffering from anxiety.

You're not alone. According to the Anxiety Disorder Association of America, 40 million Americans face this same challenge. And many are just as perplexed about how to tackle the problem as you are.

The good news is that there are tried and true ways of managing these symptoms. Some of them are easy and immediately effective. Others take a little more time and practice. But they're all about using your brain to change your brain—and to change your body, too.

This book is here to help.

It's Not Just in Your Head

Anxiety is a very real medical issue with symptoms that are mental, emotional, and physical. Mentally, you may be plagued by worries or preoccupied with fear or thoughts of dying or going crazy. Emotionally, you may feel an ambiguous but profound sense of dread, or an acute fear of panic or social situations. Physically, you may experience a racing heart, dizziness, shortness of breath, achiness, or tingling sensations.

Anxiety comes in many forms, but all affect the head *and* the body. Fortunately, bodily symptoms can be controlled by conscious effort on the part of your brain. When you get better control of those bodily symptoms, the worried mind starts to relax, too. And when you can calm your worried mind, the body relaxes in kind.

The brain is an incredibly complicated organ, far too complicated to explain here. But you can essentially think of it as having two parts—an emotional, unconscious part that feels fear, and a rational, conscious part that logically assesses things. For example, suppose you're hiking on a mountain trail when you hear rustling in the bushes. You immediately bolt down the trail, trying to escape the bear or mountain lion. Then you look back over your shoulder, see that the rustling was just another hiker, and stop your mad dash. That "run!" response was caused by your unconscious brain. Then your logical, conscious brain stepped in and said, "Look around, assess the situation! Oh, it's okay. I'm in no danger."

Anxiety works on a feedback loop. If your body gets tense, your unconscious brain notices it and says, "Oh! There must be something to worry about!" And when your unconscious brain says there must be something to worry about, your body kicks into even higher gear. And around and around it goes.

But the process also can work in reverse. You can use your conscious brain to tell your body to relax, and when your body relaxes, it tells your unconscious brain to relax, too. It's this reverse process that the techniques in this book are based on. Use them regularly, and you'll be able to turn that negative feedback loop into a positive one.

But where do you start? The first step is figuring out what kind of anxiety you may have.

If your body gets tense, your unconscious brain notices it and says, "Oh! There must be something to worry about!" . . . But the process also can work in reverse. You can use your conscious brain to tell your body to relax.

What Kind of Anxiety Do You Have?

True anxiety disorders can be diagnosed only by a trained healthcare professional. But the checklists on the following pages offer a good starting point for getting a sense of whether this book may help you. They list the typical symptoms of three common types of anxiety: panic, social anxiety, and generalized anxiety.

Which one are *you* facing?

Before you answer that question, however, it's important to consider this: Certain kinds of medical conditions—like heart problems or hormone changes—can cause symptoms identical to those of anxiety. Also, many medications can create side effects of anxiety. So before you assume you suffer from anxiety, see a physician for a checkup. Getting rid of your symptoms could be as easy as changing the dosage of one of your medications!

Certain kinds of medical conditions can cause symptoms identical to those of anxiety. So before you assume you suffer from anxiety, see a physician for a checkup.

Panic

Panic attacks are bouts of sudden, intense physical and emotional feelings of fear or terror that last for 11 to 13 minutes. They typically leave you feeling weak, exhausted, and scared for minutes or even hours after the attack subsides.

Panic attacks are bouts of sudden, intense physical and emotional feelings of fear or terror.

Have You Suffered a Panic Attack?

During the attack, did you experience:

❏ Rapid heart rate
❏ Rapid, shallow breathing
❏ Nausea
❏ Sweating

❏ Urge to urinate or diarrhea
❏ Tightness or pain in your chest
❏ Feeling that you cannot breathe or cannot catch your breath
❏ A lump in your throat or choking sensation
❏ Shaking or trembling
❏ Dizziness
❏ Feelings of unreality
❏ Belief that you are dying, going crazy, or about to lose control

If you felt five or more of these symptoms, you probably suffered a panic attack.

It's possible to experience panic attacks without suffering from panic disorder. Panic attacks are unpleasant. They are inconvenient. You aren't happy to have them. But in and of themselves, they're not a mental health disorder. It is, rather, worrying about having panic attacks and changing your life to avoid them that indicates panic disorder.

Do You Have Panic Disorder?

If you have experienced at least one panic attack, check which of the following changes you have made. Have you:

❑ Worried about having panic attacks so much that you were distracted from work or social exchanges

❑ Stopped attending activities you previously enjoyed

❑ Limited driving to roads on which you feel safe from panic

❑ Avoided transportation where you think you might panic and not be able to leave at will (e.g., a subway, bus, plane, ferry)

❑ Avoided social situations where you fear you might panic (e.g., parties, work-related engagements)

❑ Stayed out of theaters, restaurants, stadiums, or public meeting places for fear you will panic

❑ Started paying attention to exits and ways to escape a location

❑ Gone to the emergency room more than once to make sure you were not having a heart attack

❑ Avoided going into classrooms with too few or too many other students

❑ Stayed home from school for fear of having an attack

❑ Stopped shopping in stores when there are people who might observe you panicking (e.g., started grocery shopping late at night)

❑ Stopped exercising because you feared that rapid heart rate or respiration would trigger a panic attack

❏ Insisted that a family member or friend accompany you for travel, even for short distances, or accompany you into retail stores

How many did you check? If you checked:

1 = You don't have panic disorder yet, but don't make this behavior a habit! Know that you can control panic better than you can control situations or people.

2 = You're starting to change your behavior to accommodate panic. Ask yourself if giving up activities or making life more complicated is really better than managing panic.

3 = You could possibly have panic disorder. You are certainly afraid of feeling afraid, and you're changing your life to avoid panic attacks.

4 or more = Avoiding panic is controlling your life. You will benefit from learning how to stop panic attacks, and you may want some guidance to begin doing things you've been avoiding.

The problem with avoiding panic attacks is that it works. But when you change your life to avoid panic, you hand over your control to the panic. The Anxiety Busters that work best with panic are numbers 1, 2, and 5.

Social Anxiety

People who are shy know the symptoms of social anxiety in a mild way. You may not want to be the center of attention or perform in public. There's nothing wrong with being shy, and most shy people have satisfying lives without their shyness getting in the way of accomplishments. But when you have social anxiety, there are big impairments in fulfilling your potential, because you avoid experiences that could help you grow and develop your abilities.

There are three common types of symptoms for social anxiety: feeling uncomfortable being observed, anticipating being judged for social gaffes, and having mistaken beliefs.

There are three common types of symptoms for social anxiety: feeling uncomfortable being observed, anticipating being judged for social gaffes, and having mistaken beliefs.

Do You Have Social Anxiety?

Do you fear being observed while:

❏ Eating in a restaurant
❏ Signing a check or credit card receipt
❏ Answering a question at school
❏ Speaking up at a business meeting

❏   Leaving your seat during a movie or theater performance

In social situations, do you fear you will:

❏   Not be able to think of interesting things to say
❏   Not be likeable
❏   Blush or be silent when meeting new people
❏   Reveal some social inadequacy, such as wearing the wrong clothes or not knowing a "social grace" such as which fork to use at a set table
❏   Embarrass yourself by saying the wrong thing

Do you tend to:

❏   Assume others know the right way to do things
❏   Assume you're the only one who doesn't know the right answer or who has made a mistake while learning something new
❏   Believe that you will be rejected in new situations
❏   Assume that other people are watching you when you are in public
❏   Believe that feeling humiliated is inevitable and you won't be able to get over it

Of the 15 items above, how many did you check? If you checked:

2 or fewer = You do not have social anxiety disorder. Everyone feels these things from time to time.

3 = You are probably holding back from situations.

4 or more = You are too worried about your social acceptability and may be suffering social anxiety.

Is Social Anxiety Interfering With Your Life?

Your social anxieties are interfering with your life if you avoid any of the following:

❏ Going into new situations (a new club, classroom, activity)

❏ Auditioning or interviewing for positions you are qualified to hold

❏ Speaking up at a meeting

❏ Speaking up in a classroom

❏ Talking to supervisors about work-related issues

❏ Talking to people you don't know

❏ Attending gatherings of people, even to advance your career or celebrate an event

Performance anxiety is another kind of social anxiety. It's when you have anxiety in one specific social situation—such as singing in public, giving a speech, auditioning, or standing up in a classroom. Your anxiety may be intense enough to make you avoid that situation at all costs, but it is restricted to that one kind of situation.

Whether you suffer from performance anxiety or broader social anxiety, the techniques in this book can help you. The Anxiety Busters that work best with these problems are numbers 2, 5, 8, and 10.

Generalized Anxiety

Everyone worries from time to time. But people with generalized anxiety worry *a lot*, and about lots of different things. Plus, as soon as one worry gets resolved, another pops up in its place. On the drive to work you

> *People with generalized anxiety worry a lot. And about lots of different things. As soon as one worry gets resolved, another pops up in its place.*

might worry that you'll be late. When you arrive on time, you start worrying that your morning meeting won't go well. When the morning meeting goes fine, you worry that you won't finish your report by the end of the day.

Is *your* worry excessive? Take a look at the following examples and see which column seems most like your own worry.

A Worried Mind, and Body Too

Normal Worry

I'm worried about my daughter being safe on a mountain-climbing expedition.

I worry about the safety of driving in bad weather, and am very cautious on the road.

I worry about how I will pay a bill that is unexpected, and I try to figure it out.

When my kids have a physical symptom like a fever, I worry about whether it will get too high, and I watch them carefully.

I am worried before I take a test about how hard it will be and if I will get a passing grade.

Excessive Worry

Every time my daughter leaves the house, I worry that she won't return safely.

I feel intensely worried about the weather and will not drive if rain is predicted.

I worry every day about how I would manage financially if I lost my job.

I feel frantic with worry whenever my children have a fever or other physical symptom and am afraid they will die.

I worry about not being smart enough and am constantly comparing my grades to those of my friends.

Normal Worry

I worry about my spouse's drug relapse damaging our relationship permanently.

I want my children to be safe, so I research whether chemicals I use around the house could be toxic if they are ingested.

I sometimes worry if I have an unusual physical symptom, and I check it out with a doctor if the symptom does not go away in a reasonable time.

Excessive Worry

Whenever I'm in a relationship I worry about when it will end.

I'm constantly worried about whether my children will be harmed by environmental toxins, and I'm always online searching for hazards I may not be aware of.

I research all my symptoms online, no matter how minor they are, to be sure I don't have a serious disease.

If the worry in the right-hand column seems most like yours, it's worth taking a close look at whether you might have generalized anxiety.

Do You Have Generalized Anxiety?

Which of the following questions can you answer "yes" to?

❑ I worry a lot on most days, and this has been going on for 6 months or more.

❑ I ruin whole days or good events by worrying, and my worries are often unreasonable, even though they're about normal things like work, school performance, physical health, or friendships.

❑ No matter how hard I try, I cannot seem to stop the worry.

If you answered "yes" to these three questions, your anxiety is greater than normal and you may have generalized anxiety disorder.

Do You Have Physical Symptoms of Generalized Anxiety?

Do you experience:

❑ Muscle tension, including TMJ, neck pain, or backache

❑ Headaches

❑ Irritable bowel syndrome (aggravated by tension)

❑ Irritability

❑ Restless sleep or fatigue on awakening

❑ Physical jumpiness

If you have three or more of these, pay careful attention to Anxiety Busters 1 and 4. And watch for feelings of depression following prolonged worry and anxiety—there's a big overlap between depression and generalized anxiety. You may need psychotherapy help to work on those disorders.

Generalized anxiety may not seem as dramatic as panic or social anxiety, but it can still have disastrous consequences in your life. The gnawing feeling in your gut, the preoccupation and loss of attention, the sense of doom and misery, the physical agitation—all combine to prevent you from fully participating in life. Loss of pleasure and constant worry undermine both daytime activities and sleep, so you have no respite even at night. If this sounds like you, it's time to take control. The Anxiety Busters that work best with generalized anxiety are numbers 1, 6, 7, 8, and 9.

Other Types of Anxiety

There are other forms of anxiety, too. The techniques in this book may help relieve some of the symptoms of these types of anxiety, but they're mainly geared for the three we just covered. You may need to seek help from a specialist for the following problems.

Agoraphobia is a fear of public places. Some people develop agoraphobia as a result of avoiding panic attacks. Agoraphobia is sometimes so severe that people won't even leave their home. Other times people may go out but severely curtail where they go and with whom (for example, they might not go to a stadium or theater). Inability to escape is a major concern. If you have agoraphobia that started with panic, then managing panic successfully should help you undo the fear of going out. If your agoraphobia did not begin with panic, there are probably complicating factors that require psychotherapy.

A *specific phobia* is a fear of a specific thing, like snakes, spiders, or insects. Many people suffer phobias, which usually cause only minor interference with life. However, some specific phobias—like fear of the dark, driving over a bridge, or claustrophobia—can be debilitating because they interfere with many life situations. Some phobias do not seem related to any specific event that started the fear. These can usually be treated fairly easily with what are called "desensitization" methods. When the phobia is the outcome of a traumatic experience, the right treatment depends on the type of event and the kinds of repercussions still present in your life.

Post-traumatic stress disorder (PTSD) is a serious condition. It's the result of an experience that threatened your life or the life of someone else in your presence, that created a sense of terror, or that was out of your control (as in a natural disaster, war, or crime). Not everyone gets PTSD as a result of such experiences, but those who do may experience nightmares or flashbacks, get depressed or anxious, have trouble concentrating or sleeping, and become easily agitated or even rageful. Although all of the techniques discussed in this book will help manage symptoms of the anxiety accompanying PTSD, they won't resolve the traumatic experience. If you think you may suffer from PTSD, consult a therapist. Help is available!

Obsessive-compulsive disorder (OCD) is marked by unreasonable worries and obsessive fears. These obsessive fears may cause a person to develop ritualistic behaviors called "compulsions" to try to relieve the anxiety caused by the obsessive thoughts. Some compulsions, like repeated hand washing, are obvious, but others are much more subtle, such as touching a talisman or leaving the house on the same foot every time you walk out. The techniques in this book that focus on the body—Anxiety Busters 1 through 4—will help people with OCD, but the ones that focus on changing your thought patterns will not. The Obsessive-Compulsive Foundation website is a good resource for signs, symptoms, and treatment ideas.

Isn't There Just a Magic Pill?

When you're lying in bed at 3 A.M., staring at the ceiling as worries swirl around in your head, or when you're gripped with fear at the mere thought of driving to see your new nephew, or when your heart starts pounding before you even arrive at your best friend's birthday party, it can be easy to wish for a magic pill to set you at ease. It's true that medication can help alleviate symptoms of anxiety, and insurance and drug companies consider it a first-line treatment. But these drugs often have unpleasant side effects, and your symptoms will reemerge when you stop using them. Medication is just one option of many.

> *Medication can help alleviate symptoms of anxiety. But these drugs often have unpleasant side effects, and your symptoms will reemerge when you stop using them.*

Recent neurobiology research has transformed our understanding of anxiety disorders. We now know that anxiety is generated by specific problems with brain structure and function. This means you have great power to use your brain to change your brain—by consciously changing aspects of your lifestyle, thought, and behavior. This can work just as well as medication, and the effects can last longer. We already have a built-in, God-given tool for soothing anxiety—and it doesn't cost a dime!

A Personal Note From the Author

For many years I experienced panic attacks and bouts of dreadful worry. I know firsthand just how awful they feel! It wasn't until early in my career as a therapist that I found, by luck and by studying, techniques that helped me get rid of the anxiety. I began using them with my clients, too. Many years later, advances in neurobiology helped us understand why these techniques work. Luckily, though, you don't need to understand the "why" to find relief from your symptoms.

I wrote this book because I want you to benefit from what I've learned. I've honed and refined these Anxiety Busters over my four decades of helping clients with symptoms just like yours. And it gives me great pleasure to see them work.

Three's a Charm: Body, Mind, and Behavior

When you suffer from anxiety, it shows up in your body, in your thoughts, and in your behaviors. The first four Anxiety Busters in this book are aimed at relieving your physical symptoms of anxiety. The next four are about soothing your anxious mind. And the last two will help you change your anxious behaviors. Use them together, and you've got a comprehensive plan that will calm you on all three fronts.

Each of the Busters includes several different ways to achieve your desired goal. This means you can pick and choose which approach will work best for you. And don't feel like you have to do the techniques in order. Just select the one that works best for you and go from there.

Now let's get started!

Avoid CATS (Not the Furry Ones)

MARK PACED BACK and forth across the kitchen. His cell phone sat on the counter, silent. Where *was* she? His wife always called when she was going to be late. He opened the refrigerator and got another beer. Empty bottles stood among the takeout boxes of half-eaten Chinese food next to the sink.

Suddenly the phone sounded with an incoming text message. Mark leaped to pick it up. It was a message from his coworker Catherine, reminding him to bring in the paperwork for the Collins account tomorrow. It was almost 11 P.M. Mark dialed Emily's number again, but her phone went straight to voice mail. Her "girls night out" was probably just running late, Mark told himself. She didn't get home until midnight the last time she went out with them. But what if something had happened? What if she'd had a car accident? What if the girls had gone out after the movie and were sipping martinis with some group of obnoxious Wall Street types? Mark couldn't get the image of Emily flirting with one of those jerks out of his head.

He rummaged through the drawer where he kept his cigarettes until he found an open pack. The television in the living room was still on. He sat down on the couch, lit a cigarette, and started flipping through the channels.

At 11:30, Emily's key clicked open the front door lock.

Confronted with Mark's situation, anyone might be nervous. But his overreaction wasn't being helped by the lifestyle he'd recently slipped into.

Your body has to process whatever you take in, whether it's food, substances like tobacco and alcohol, or a demanding, distracting environment. CATS stands for caffeine, alcohol,

CATS stands for caffeine, alcohol, tobacco, and sugar/ sweeteners. Calming the anxious body starts with changing your intake of all of them—and with limiting stimulation from your surroundings.

tobacco, and sugar/sweeteners. Calming the anxious body starts with changing your intake of all of them—and with limiting stimulation from your surroundings.

Cut Down on Caffeine

Caffeine may seem like a relatively harmless substance, but research has shown that it can trigger out-of-the-blue panic. Even fairly small amounts of caffeine—as little as a cup of coffee a day—can bring on an attack. But caffeine does more than just trigger panic. People who have generalized anxiety are typically physically tense, and those tension levels increase with the intake of caffeine. And the flushing, sweating, and shakiness of social anxiety are made worse by caffeine, too, because it heightens the arousal of the nervous system.

Make an effort to notice the amounts of caffeine in the everyday products you use—soda, coffee, tea, chocolate, and energy drinks or tablets. It's easy to find the milligrams of caffeine in these products on the Internet. People vary widely in their tolerance to caffeine. If you keep track of your changes in mood, tension, and anxiety after consuming it, you'll quickly be able to find your limit and alter your intake accordingly.

Avoid Alcohol

Frank Sinatra is rumored to have said, "Alcohol may be man's worst enemy, but the Bible says love your enemy." Many people use alcohol as a way to reduce stress, handle fear, and avoid unpleasant emotional states. A moderate amount of alcohol can quickly and temporarily induce a relaxed state of mind or body. However, the impact of alcohol on the anxious body is more complicated than it initially seems.

People under stress tend to consume alcohol in larger quantities or with more frequency than they might otherwise. At times of unremitting stress—such as during a divorce, a particularly difficult project that requires long hours of work, or caring for a family member who is ill—you may use more alcohol. All of these situations can interfere with relaxing or getting to sleep, and alcohol may help induce sleep. Alcohol can also ameliorate social fears. It can make you feel less anxious about facing a social demand, like attending an office party or dinner engagement.

But although alcohol may temporarily help you relax, it is actually a profound anxiety-*causing* agent. When it's eliminated from the body by your liver, alcohol actually leaves nerves in an agitated state. People who have a couple of drinks at night may find it easier to get drowsy and fall asleep, but they often awaken halfway through the night and can't get back to sleep. This is because the alcohol is leaving the nervous system in an agitated state. The best solution to middle-of-the-night awakening, if you're not going to eliminate alcohol altogether, is to restrict alcohol consumption to earlier in the evening, so this phase of detoxification is complete before you head to bed.

> *When it's eliminated from the body by your liver, alcohol actually leaves nerves in an agitated state.*

Herbal teas are a better bedtime relaxant. Find ones with calming properties, such as kava, chamomile, catnip, lemon balm, hops, and valerian. The herbs in these teas help soothe the brain and promote sleep with no hangover effects in the morning.

One way of identifying the impact of alcohol on your body is to keep an anxiety or panic record. Keep track of how much alcohol you drink at night, and record your overall level of anxiety or occurrence of panic the next day. Regularly maintaining this record over the course of a few months will tell you a lot about how alcohol affects your system.

If you have trouble giving up or limiting your alcohol intake, you may need to seek help for addiction. Alcohol addiction requires separate treatment from anxiety management—it won't disappear just because you can control your anxiety. Help with addiction is available, whether it's a 12-step program or other form of help. Check www.aa.org for resources.

Track Your Tobacco Use

The rituals of tobacco use—lighting up the cigarette, pipe, or cigar, or the act of chewing—are often strongly associated with creating a space of calm and separation from stress. If you smoke, you may feel that it gives you time to step out, relax, think, and soothe yourself. But smoking has many anxiety-provoking effects, too—sensations of dizziness, tingling, shortness of breath, or just the nagging thought that you should not be smoking because of the health concerns associated with it.

Of course, there's probably no faster way to make you anxious than to decide you have to quit smoking! So for now, just try tracking the relationship between your sensations of anxiety and your use of tobacco. You can't know exactly how smoking affects you until you track your reactions to it. A smoking record can be as simple as the one shown here. Rate your anxiety before, during, and after each cigarette (or other form of tobacco), regardless of how many you smoke.

Cigarette	#1	#2	#3	#4	#5
Anxiety before smoking					
Anxiety while smoking					
Anxiety after smoking					

One therapy client of mine found that when he quit smoking, he no longer felt that constant edge of anxiety that made him fear that he was about to panic. Others have said that smoking decreases their anxiety while they're doing it, but increases it afterward.

A good way to change your tobacco intake is to do a breathing relaxer before you light up (Anxiety Buster 2). These exercises can help relieve your underlying anxiety . and make you feel less compelled to pick up the cigarette in the first place. Another option is what I call "Break Into Your Cigarette Break." Think of something relaxing, like stretching or getting up from your desk to look out the window for a moment, and do that before you pick up the cigarette. If you still want the cigarette after that, go ahead and have it, but use it for the nicotine, not for the relaxation break.

> *A good way to change your tobacco intake is to do a breathing relaxer before you light up.*

Steer Clear of Sugars and Sweeteners

Sugar and artificial sweeteners can cause a variety of anxiety problems. Certain foods are especially a problem for people who have hypoglycemia, or low blood sugar. When someone with hypoglycemia eats foods that turn to sugar quickly— simple carbohydrates like a doughnut or plate of pasta—the level of blood sugar rises quickly. Soon after, it plummets, causing symptoms that feel very much like anxiety, such as sweating, flushing, nausea, and shakiness. A good way to counteract this problem is to eat complex carbohydrates rather than simple ones, balance your meals with protein, and minimize caffeine.

Artificial sweeteners, aspartame in particular, are a trickier subject because opinion on them is divided, but some studies have shown a connection between increased anxiety and aspartame.

As with the other CATS substances, it's a good idea to simply track your anxiety levels after using aspartame or sugar. If you notice an increase in your symptoms, it makes sense to use less or eliminate it.

Eat and Sleep Well

You are what you eat: It may be a cliché, but science has proven it's true. Your brain needs certain chemicals to function properly, and it makes those chemicals out of the nutrients in the food you eat. Remember that *what* you eat is more important than *how much* you eat. Dark green, leafy vegetables will help build new brain cells, and the

> *Your brain needs certain chemicals to function properly, and it makes those chemicals out of the nutrients in the food you eat.*

colorful orange, red, and yellow vegetables and fresh fruits will give you the other vitamins you need. A small amount of protein three times a day will promote the production of important chemicals, and healthy fats from olive oil and fish have a good reputation for helping your brain do its work. It's best to get nutrients from food itself, but vitamin supplements can be a good idea if you're lacking in some areas.

Then, get some sleep! Most people need about 8 hours. Your body uses sleeping time to repair and grow new cells—including those in your brain. And remember those nutrients that your brain uses to make important chemicals? Well, it

> *Your body uses sleeping time to repair and grow new cells—including those in your brain.*

takes 12 to 15 hours for your body to digest your food and send the nutrients to your brain—which means breakfast is essential to brain health! If you have trouble sleeping (as many people with anxiety do), be sure to read Anxiety Buster 4. It has some helpful tips for getting a good night's sleep.

Take a Break!

We live in an increasingly stimulating world. Our phones ding and ring—day and night—with endless e-mails, text messages, tweets, and calls. Our computers are usually open and on all day, both at home and at work. Our bosses often expect us to be on call, or at least checking e-mail, even during our off hours. "Oh?" they say with an arched eyebrow. "You didn't get the message? I sent you an e-mail at 9 o'clock last night to tell you the meeting this morning would start an hour early."

If you're a student, you may be navigating crowded, fluorescent-lit hallways cluttered with flat-screen monitors showing news feeds on school events or the weather. You're eating meals in noisy school cafeterias. You're trying to keep track of the demands of your teachers, friends, coaches, club leaders, and the like. Your inbox is full of "important" notifications about everything from class registration deadlines and the final exam schedule to where that upcoming lecture, "Vernacular Architecture of 16th-Century Bydgoszcz," is taking place.

Then there's the stressful commute to work or school, battling traffic or squeezing into packed subways, trains, or buses.

And if you have kids, you're dealing with the constant demands of parenting on top of all that.

You may say you're great at multitasking, and you may be right. Lots of people have learned to juggle multiple activities and navigate a high-stimulation environment. But these constant demands take their toll and make us more susceptible to anxiety.

Technology-Free Times

Every time the computer or phone dings to tell us there is a waiting message, our brains register an alert, hearing the sound as a demand for attention. That alert is not calmed until we respond to it. And if we don't respond right away, it takes mental energy to push away the urge to respond. That tension may be subtle, but it keeps your brain revved up and ready to be anxious about any number of unrelated things.

To reduce the impact of this techno-stress, make a deliberate choice to create technology-free times. Look at the following list of suggestions and pick out just one to try for at least a full week. (You can add more after you get comfortable with the one you pick first.)

- Wait to check e-mail for at least an hour into your workday. Try getting some work done first.
- Set your phone on silent and let calls go to voice mail. Check your voice mail and return calls at specific times that suit your schedule. (On your outgoing message, you can let callers know when they can expect a return call.)
- Turn off things that ring and ding while you are focusing on work.
- Turn off everything at home that rings, including cell phones, while you eat your meal. Make mealtimes a no-call zone.
- Leave your cell phone in the car when you go to a restaurant, or at least turn the ringer to silent (not vibrate) so that your attention is completely on your meal and your companions.
- If you carry a pager for work, make sure you take it off when you are not on call, and do not encourage people to page you as a means of reaching you when you are not on call.

- Don't mix personal and work-related numbers, so that you can elect not to answer the work phone without missing family or friends' calls. Don't answer work calls on personal time.
- Make a specific agreement with your supervisor about exactly which hours you are expected to work. Don't respond to messages from work except during those hours.

After you've picked one of these ideas, rate your anxiety level each day before, during, and after the technology-free time. You may find that the technology-free time actually causes *more* anxiety when you first begin trying it, but be patient! After a week of practice—and realizing that waiting to check the phone doesn't result in a major catastrophe—you'll notice a difference.

The Two-Minute Vacation

How would you describe your workplace or school environment? Is it calm and quiet, or noisy and distracting? Many people aren't even aware that the noise of an open office or a dormitory is affecting their stress level. But your body has to constantly block out those distractions, and this can heighten your anxiety.

Try some of these breaks at least every 90 minutes at work or while studying:

- Stand up, stretch, and take a moment to look out the window.
- Go outside, even for just a couple of minutes.
- Have a picture of your favorite people or place handy, and when you look at it, take a moment to feel deep appreciation and love.
- Walk up and down a hallway, take a drink of water, or take a trip to the bathroom, even if you don't need it.
- Close your eyes and imagine a place you love. Then run through what you experience there in each of your five senses. By the time you've set the scene, it will be about 2 minutes, and you can come back to the present with the feeling that you've had a small break.

You can also make up your own mini vacation on the spot, whenever you feel like you need a break. Getting irritable after hours of running errands? Take time to sit down for a cup of tea or a snack. Ready to snap at your rambunctious children? Ask them to play outside for a while. Feeling restless at a cocktail party? Step outside a moment to look at the night sky. Stepping away from the stimulation even just briefly will help calm your nerves.

MARK WAS AT the front door, glowering, before Emily had even completely opened it. "Where have you been?!" he asked, not waiting for a reply. "I tried calling you a million times!"

Emily looked startled and pulled her phone out of her coat pocket. "Oh, sorry. I forgot to switch it back on after we got out of the movie." She dropped her purse on a chair and walked into the living room as Mark angrily opened another beer.

The living room stank of cigarettes. "Have you been smoking in the house?" Emily looked at Mark incredulously. "It reeks in here!"

Mark ignored the question. "I asked you where you've been."

"Mark, you *know* where I was." Emily opened a window to air out the room. "What's up with you? You're acting weird. You've been acting weird since you got that Collins account."

"Don't change the subject," Mark snapped. "You should've called to say you were gonna be late."

Emily sighed and rubbed her head. "First of all, Mark, I'm not late." She checked her watch. "It's a quarter to twelve. Second, you're drunk." She slipped off her shoes and headed to the bedroom. "We can talk about this in the morning."

Mark sat back down on the couch and began flipping through the channels again. He knew Emily was right— ever since things at work had heated up, he'd been on edge. He was drinking three times as much coffee as he used to, and by the end of the day he was so wired that it took three or four beers to get to sleep. Something had to change.

The next day after work, Mark and Emily sat down to come up with a plan. She would make a point of cooking healthy dinners—no more takeout. And he would limit himself to two cups of coffee, both before noon. He could have a few beers when he was out with friends, but none at home. They would also get up early each day to go for a run before they headed off to work.

Sticking to the plan wasn't easy, but things were markedly better after a couple months of the new routine. Mark was drinking less and had almost completely quit smoking, and he felt more focused at work. The morning runs with Emily had become his favorite part of the day—they both left their phones at home when they went out, and just enjoyed the sunrise and being out in the brisk air. By the time they got back from the run, Mark felt calm and energized and ready to start the day.

ANXIETY BUSTER 2

Breathe

ISAAC AND SHANNON were the first to arrive in the conference room. A platter of fresh fruit sat on the table, and bottles of water had been placed in front of each chair. Isaac plucked a few grapes and popped them in his mouth.

"Hard to believe we're actually here," he said under his breath as he looked around the room. He and Shannon had been best friends in college. When they discovered, just a couple of months after graduating, that they'd both applied for the same writing position at a popular arts and entertainment magazine, they each swore they'd be happy no matter which of them got the job. Now here they were together—and working as a team no less—

thanks to the magazine's decision to hire them both. It was a dream come true.

Shannon laid their folder of notes on the table. "Okay, I think we're presenting second." She shuffled through the pages. "Are you still good with introducing our idea and then having me go into the details?"

Isaac nodded and sat down as their coworkers began filing into the room.

The editor in chief took a seat at the head of the table and put on her reading glasses. "Okay, let's go ahead and get started if we're all here. Philip, I think you're first."

Philip launched into his presentation, with others at the table asking questions and making suggestions. But as Isaac listened, something strange happened—everything around him began to feel vaguely surreal, as if he were just dreaming the whole thing. His coworkers at the table seemed to be interacting as if they were in a play and Isaac was the audience.

What's going on? Isaac thought. His heart began to race. He glanced at the clock. Ten past three.

Suddenly he felt like he couldn't breathe. His mouth went dry. Now his heart *really* began to race. Philip was wrapping up his presentation. Isaac felt like he might pass out. He picked up his pen and scribbled at the top of his notes: SICK. YOU TAKE OVER. He passed the paper to Shannon, got up, and walked unsteadily out of the room.

In the hallway, Isaac leaned against the wall. He still couldn't manage to catch his breath, and his chest felt tight. Was he having a heart attack? It didn't seem possible, but something was definitely wrong.

An intern walking down the hall saw him and stopped. "Are you okay?" She looked alarmed.

"No. I mean, I don't think so," Isaac stammered. "I don't know." Sweat streamed down the sides of his face.

"I'm calling an ambulance," the girl said, reaching for her cell phone.

"No!" Isaac blurted, imagining the scene that would cause.

"Well, you need to get to a hospital," she insisted. She paused a moment and then dialed a car service. A few minutes later, Isaac was on his way to the emergency room.

Oh, sure—just breathe, you may be thinking. I *don't need a book to tell me that!* But the truth is that anxiety may be affecting your breathing in ways you're not even aware of. And learning to control your breath is the single best way to control the physical side of anxiety. Plus, the beauty of breathing is that it works even if you don't believe it's going to.

So how does it work?

Panic begins with unconscious activity in your brain that sparks the sudden rise of heart rate and respiration. Once those physical reactions start, the feedback loop begins—your brain notices the physical symptoms, gets alarmed, and sends a message to your body to even further increase your heart rate and breathing.

The beauty of breathing is that it works even if you don't believe it's going to.

But the good thing is that your body can't rev up and slow down at the same time. So when you make a conscious decision to breathe slowly, the rest of your body starts to slow down, too, and those panicky feelings subside.

Your body can't rev up and slow down at the same time. So when you make a conscious decision to breathe slowly, the rest of your body starts to slow down, too.

The sensation of generalized anxiety is also caused by unconscious activity. You may feel a sense of dread or impending trouble. You may have tension building even when you're not aware of it—until you feel tied in knots. This kind of physical experience of anxiety causes you to have a physical reaction, and conscious breathing can be used to calm it.

Assess Your Breathing

The next time you're under pressure, set aside a part of your attention to observe how your breathing changes. If you have to speak at a meeting, notice your breathing. If you're having a disagreement, watch how your breath changes. Even if you're just feeling time pressure, take a moment to feel your breathing. It may surprise you to find that you've been holding your breath or breathing shallowly or unevenly.

How Am I Breathing?

How does your breathing change when you're under pressure? Check off each of the following that apply.

❑ Short or blocked intake
❑ Gasping
❑ Long in, short out
❑ Shallow
❑ Gulping
❑ Even, but fast
❑ Holding breath
❑ Panting
❑ Hyperventilating

Diaphragmatic Breathing

Taking just one deep breath and letting it go will help relieve some stress, but breathing to control anxiety works better if you do a method called "diaphragmatic breathing." Practice the first time by lying down or standing—after that, you can breathe anywhere without anyone noticing. Remember, the goal is not to change the way you breathe as you go about your daily activities, but rather to consciously change the way you breathe when you begin to feel panic or anxiety coming on.

Here's how to do it:

1. Lie down flat on your back or stand in a relaxed manner, feet slightly apart, knees loose. This is so you can sense the movement in your abdomen, which should move *out* when you inhale and pull *in* when you exhale.
2. Rest your hand on your abdomen. This will help you notice if you are breathing deeply enough and whether your chest is tight.
3. Next, exhale the air in your lungs so they are completely empty.
4. Then breathe in, evenly, through your nose. Fill your lungs

from bottom to top in equal, even amounts. Imagine how a balloon fills with water when you attach it to a faucet. The bottom fills and widens first, and then the water expands the upper portion. The air should go into your lungs in the same way. Again, make sure the inhalation is slow and even. It may help to count until you feel exactly full—a slow 1, 2, 3, 4. You'll probably take three to six counts to fill completely. If you don't like the idea of counting, breathe while thinking a sentence with an even rhythm, such as "I am steadily filling my lungs with air. I am emptying my lungs slowly and evenly."

5. Exhale evenly, taking longer than you did to inhale, at a slow pace until your lungs feel empty. Imagine you are blowing at the flame of a candle enough to move it but not blow it out.

6. If you get dizzy, exhale for two counts longer or pause for two counts at the end of the exhalation of your breath before you start to inhale again.

7. Continue the slow, even inhalation and exhalation for about a minute, but over time gradually increase the breathing practice to 5 minutes.

Practice!

Most people who panic immediately forget their panic control measures unless they've practiced them. It's essential to use diaphragmatic breathing the moment you sense a panic attack beginning, so you must practice frequently to be ready. There are apps for your phone—like Breathe2Relax, Relax Lite, and MyCalmBeat—that can measure and track your breathing. Consider using any one of the several that are available for free or small fees. After you've tried the diaphragmatic breathing exercise at home, practice it 10 or more times a day, for a minute each time, whenever you're waiting for something. Do this for 30 days. Remember, you don't need to be standing or lying down. You can do this whenever you are:

- Stopped at a stoplight
- On hold on the phone
- Waiting in line at a store
- Watching the commercials during a television show
- Waiting for the microwave to heat some food
- Waiting for a friend at work or school
- Waiting in the car to pick someone up
- Waiting for a computer program to load

Most people who panic immediately forget their panic control measures unless they've practiced them.

- Waiting for the teacher to hand out the test papers
- Waiting for a meeting to start

Diaphragmatic Breathing to Control Panic Attacks

You can control panic in two ways. The first is to identify the signs that you are about to panic, and start breathing that very second. This way, you can avert the attack.

The other is learning to slow and stop panic that's already underway. Doing this requires a longer period of breathing—at least 5 minutes. The following exercise will get you ready for this extended breathing time.

After practicing diaphragmatic breathing for 7 days, pick one time of day when you can predict that you will be uninterrupted for a few minutes. During this one uninterrupted period, you're going to add 1 minute of breathing at a time.

Begin by setting a timer for 2 minutes (you can do this on most of the phone apps that are available), and when you can breathe for 2 minutes, set it for 3 minutes the next time. Learn to sustain diaphragmatic breathing for a minimum of 5 minutes. Again, you need at least 5 minutes to slow and stop a panic attack that is underway.

Breathing to Calm Down in Other Situations

Getting ready to board an airplane during a thunderstorm? Sitting down to take a final exam in class? Meeting someone for a blind date? Basic diaphragmatic breathing can help you calm down before any situation that makes you tense.

A particularly good 1-minute exercise is the In 2, Out 2-4-6-8-10 method. It goes like this:

1. Inhale to the count of 2.
2. Exhale to the count of 2.
3. Inhale to the count of 2.
4. Exhale to the count of 4.
5. Inhale to the count of 2.
6. Exhale to the count of 6.
7. Inhale to the count of 2.
8. Exhale to the count of 8.
9. Inhale to the count of 2.
10. Exhale to the count of 10.

When you're dealing with hectic or emotionally trying situations from which you need a break but can only get a short time away, the 5-Count Energizing Breath works well. It's hard to do subtly, though, so a good option is to leave the room or go to the restroom. In fact, if you are washing your hands it is ideal to do this breathing method and shake water off your hands with five short shakes on the exhale.

1. Inhale smoothly to a quick count of 5.
2. Exhale by huffing your breath out in short bursts to the count of 5: huh-huh-huh-huh-huh.

After breathing off the tense energy you have accumulated, you can reenter the situation with less tension and more energy to cope.

Obstacles to Diaphragmatic Breathing

Diaphragmatic breathing is a powerful way to disrupt panic and anxiety, but sometimes people have difficulty learning it. Following are a few common obstacles to diaphragmatic breathing, along with ways of getting around them.

- People with breathing problems such as asthma should consider eliminating the counting altogether. For those who do not like the idea of counting, breathe while thinking a sentence with an even rhythm, such as, "I am steadily filling my lungs with air. I am emptying my lungs slowly and evenly." Fill up evenly, with no gulps or gasps, so the top is reached physically (in your image of the balloon) just in time to release the breath at the same even, measured pace.

- Some people get anxious when they start to breathe deeply. If this sounds like you, try limiting your breathing to a minute at a time, reminding yourself it's only 1 minute. When that's completely comfortable, add 30-second intervals. If your anxiety continues, you might want to consult a therapist. Anxiety with breathing is sometimes a problem for people who hold their breath to avoid feeling emotions, and you may need support to face that issue.

- It's very rare for diaphragmatic breathing to have no positive impact on panic reduction, but some people report that breathing does not seem to help. Have someone observe how you are breathing, and redo the assessment to see if you are inadvertently resorting to one of those ways of breathing.

- Some people have difficulty concentrating on breathing. Here is the best way to handle this:
  - Notice that you have been distracted and mentally say to yourself, "Oh. A thought." Just notice, with no judgment against yourself for being distracted. Don't get upset with yourself or impatient with the breathing. Consider thoughts as clouds in the sky, just drifting by.

You have no need to stop them, examine them, or be irritated that they are there.

— Redirect your attention to your breath. Focus on the physical sensation of breathing—the feeling of your lungs expanding, the sensation of feeling your waistband or of how your back shifts against a chair. Feel the breath move through your nostrils or out of your mouth.

— Count to measure the pace to help keep your focus on the breath.

A Last Word About Diaphragmatic Breathing

Breathing correctly is simple to do but not easy to master. And if it's going to effectively reduce tension, you first have to remember to use it! Until it becomes a habit, you may forget to breathe under anxiety or tension. It takes some time for this process to become smooth and easy. But once you've mastered it, you've got a powerful tool for stopping the physical symptoms of anxiety dead in their tracks.

THE DOCTOR WHO saw Isaac at the hospital was kind and thorough. She did a physical exam and ran some tests, but she suspected that Isaac's physical health was fine, and sent him home with a brochure on panic attacks and diaphragmatic breathing methods. Sure enough, all the test results came back normal a few days later.

By the time the next editorial board meeting rolled around, Isaac had a month's worth of breathing practice under his belt.

"I hope you took your Valium this time," Shannon joked as they entered the conference room.

Isaac forced a laugh. As he pulled out his chair, he consciously exhaled all the air from his lungs. Once seated, he began a long breath inward through his nose, counting to 4 as he inhaled. Then the exhalation again, to a count of 6, as the others took their seats. The editor in chief started the meeting with a few general remarks about the upcoming issue. Everything was fine. Isaac felt a little nervous, but his heart wasn't racing and he didn't feel like he was choking.

"So, I believe you're first on the agenda." The editor in chief directed her gaze at Isaac. "What have you guys got for us?"

Isaac inhaled slowly, smiled, and began.

ANXIETY BUSTER

Use Mindfulness With Shifting Awareness

Tisha's eyes welled with tears as she clicked through Ross's Facebook images. It hadn't been more than a few months since he'd moved out, and already he was with someone new, the two of them smiling at the camera as they lounged on a beach in Bali. It was her own fault, Tisha told herself. Ross had spent the last five years begging her to get out more, and when that didn't work, he'd suggested counseling, which she also dragged her feet on. Finally he'd gotten fed up, and who could blame him?

Tisha had always been shy, even as a child. In college she had a few close friends, but her idea of a fun night was staying in and watching a movie, not hitting the campus parties. When she met Ross a few years later, he seemed like the perfect match. Warm and outgoing, he had a large network of friends, and Tisha could engage with them through him. Now, though, they were all gone, along with Ross. Tisha felt like a failure: 40 years old, single, and with no real friends of her own.

Her isolation had crept up on her slowly. She'd kept in touch with friends from school for a few years, and she occasionally went out with colleagues after work. But social events exhausted her, and when she'd begun freelancing from home instead of working at the office a few years ago, she lost touch with the few people she did regularly see. Gradually her world narrowed, revolving around long hours at home on the computer, cooking dinner for Ross, and going to bed after watching a couple hours of television. That life had felt safe—Tisha didn't have to worry about making some social gaffe, which she always seemed to do when she was out, and she didn't have to endure the stress of small talk with people she didn't know well. But now that Ross was gone, she had no one.

Tisha put her head in her hands and sobbed. She had to reach out to someone. Her eyes still blurry from tears, she clicked over to the page of her old college friend Stephanie and composed a quick message: "Hey, Stephanie. It's been a while! Just thought I'd say hi. . . . Ross and I split up."

Stephanie replied the next day. Soon Tisha had spilled the whole story: how hurt she was about Ross's new girlfriend, how she rarely left the house, how the thought of meeting new people—or even old acquaintances—made her sick to her stomach with worry. Stephanie, always the problem solver and eager to help when she was needed, spent a sleepless night doing online research, eventually hitting on social anxiety and ways of managing it.

Anxiety, by nature, is focused on what was or what will be. It is rarely focused on the moment. If something bad is happening right now, you're probably not anxious or worried about it—rather, you're probably just dealing with it. You may be scared, but there's a difference between actively dealing with a situation while you are scared and being anxious or worried about something in the past or future.

Mindfulness is a way of being fully present in the moment you are living in. Such presence is the antithesis of anxiety. Various applications of mindfulness and medi-

> *Mindfulness is a way of being fully present in the moment you are living in. Such presence is the antithesis of anxiety.*

tation have developed rapidly over the past few years, but one in particular—Mindfulness With Shifting Awareness—is very helpful for managing anxiety.

People with panic disorder are highly vigilant to the physical signs of panic starting—increased heart rate, increased respiration, and so on. People with social anxiety are similarly attuned to physical sensations. When they begin flushing, sweating, or shaking, they worry that other people will see these physical reactions and judge them negatively. People with generalized anxiety often plunge into worry by focusing on sensations of dread that are really just the byproduct of brain chemistry and not due to any real danger or problem. Whenever you focus on such sensations, you doom yourself to having the physical reaction you fear.

Do *you* overfocus on your bodily sensations? The next time you get panicky, feel socially anxious, or feel dread that you turn into worry, ask yourself these questions:

- Did I feel the physical sensations (e.g., dread, panic, queasiness) first?
- Did I worry about whether those sensations would get worse?
- Did they get worse?

- Did I then start to really worry, have a panic attack, or get flushed and sweaty?

If this sounds like you, you'll benefit from Mindfulness With Shifting Awareness. Over time, this one exercise will help you ignore those fleeting and inconsequential sensations of anxiety. How does it do this? The technique will:

- Give you a sense of control. By focusing attention on what is happening around you, you gain some sense of control over how you are experiencing the moment. You are choosing what to attend to.
- Enhance your ability to observe yourself. Knowing what you're feeling is the first step in stopping those sensations.
- Help you ignore disturbing physical sensations. When you intentionally turn your focus from one thing (a physical sensation) to another (observations of the outer world), you calm yourself.

Use Mindfulness With Shifting Awareness

It's helpful to do this technique for the first time with a partner who can lead you through the exercise while you devote attention to your own awareness and don't have to divide it by reading the instructions. If you can't find a partner, record yourself slowly reading aloud the following instructions and play back the tape (or the audio file on your smartphone) as you do the exercise.

1. With eyes closed, follow your breath into your body as you inhale through your nose. Notice each sensation of inhaling.
    - Notice the coolness of the air.
    - Notice the pressure of airflow.
    - Notice how the movement feels through your nose, throat, trachea, and into your lungs.
    - Notice the feeling of your body shifting against your clothing and the chair you are sitting on.
    - Follow the breath out of your body, exhaling through your nose or mouth.
    - Notice the warmth of the air.
    - Notice the pressure of airflow reversed past your throat, sinuses, and nose or mouth.
    - Notice how the movement of air feels through your lungs, trachea, throat, and nose or mouth.
    - Notice the change in the feeling of your body shifting against your clothing and the chair you are sitting on.

2. Exhale your awareness to the world around you without opening your eyes.

    - Direct your awareness to every sound in the environment, paying special attention to location and intensity.
    - Shift your awareness to the smells in the environment.
    - Shift your awareness to the sense of movement in the environment if you are in a place with other people nearby.

3. Now, shift awareness back to your body, and inhale again.

    - Notice the coolness of the air.
    - Notice the pressure of airflow.
    - Notice how the movement feels through your nose, throat, trachea, and into your lungs.
    - Notice the feeling of your body shifting against your clothing and the chair you are sitting on.
    - Add this awareness: Feel your heart beating.
    - As you exhale, notice the warmth of the air.
    - Notice the pressure of the airflow reversed past your throat, sinuses, and nose or mouth.
    - Notice how the movement of air feels through your lungs, trachea, throat, and nose or mouth.
    - Notice the change in the feeling of your body shifting against your clothing and the chair you are sitting on.

4. Now, with eyes remaining shut, exhale your awareness into the room.

   - Direct your awareness to every sound in the environment, paying special attention to location and intensity.
   - Shift your awareness to the smells in the environment.
   - Shift your awareness to the sense of movement in the environment if you are in a place with other people nearby.

5. Now, shift your awareness back to your body as you inhale.

   - Notice the coolness of the air.
   - Notice the pressure of airflow.
   - Notice how the movement feels through your nose, throat, trachea, and lungs.
   - Notice the feeling of your body shifting against your clothing and the chair you are sitting on.
   - Feel your heart beating.
   - Add this awareness: Feel the movement of blood or energy through your body or limbs.
   - Notice the warmth of the air.
   - Notice the pressure of the airflow reversed past your throat, sinuses, and nose or mouth.
   - Notice how the movement of air feels through your lungs, trachea, throat, and nose or mouth.

- Notice the change in the feeling of your body shifting against your clothing and the chair you are sitting on.

6. One more time, shift your awareness to the external world as you exhale.
   - Direct your awareness to every sound in the environment, paying special attention to location and intensity.
   - Shift your awareness to the smells in the environment.
   - Shift your awareness to the sense of movement in the environment if you are in a place with other people nearby.

7. Prepare to open your eyes by becoming aware of light coming through your eyelids, and then gradually allow your eyes to open, taking in the color of the light and then the things you can observe with your vision as you become fully present and aware of the situation you are in.

The more you practice this exercise in a calm, controlled setting, the better you'll be at using it in situations that make you nervous. When you apply the technique in those real-life situations, you don't need to close your eyes or go

The more you practice this exercise in a calm, controlled setting, the better you'll be at using it in situations that make you nervous.

through all the steps. Because you've practiced, you'll already have a good sense of how to smoothly shift your awareness inward or outward.

Using the Technique With Panic Attacks

When you have panic disorder, physical sensations may trigger worry that an attack is headed your way. By using this technique to focus on the external world, you can avoid triggering your own panic.

If you have the occasional out-of-the-blue attack, use the technique to immediately breathe and shift your focus away from physical sensations. This will ward it off.

If you feel a panic attack coming on before you're fully practiced in breathing or mindfulness, the attack may indeed develop. But don't despair! With practice, you'll eventually get a handle on managing your panic. Until then, remember that you don't need to be afraid of panic happening—it won't last long, and although it's unpleasant, it's not lethal.

Using the Technique With Social Anxiety

One of the best ways to ward off the flushing, sweating, and shaking symptoms of social anxiety is to learn how to discreetly stay calm in situations that could provoke anxiety.

Mindfulness with shifting awareness can take you either inward or outward, depending on which is the most helpful direction at the moment. Staying focused on inner breathing rather than on the surrounding hubbub can help shy people avoid the overstimulation that triggers blushing, sweating, or flushing. And focusing outward can help you ignore your physical signs of nervousness, breaking the vicious cycle of sweating leading to even more sweating and shaky hands leading to shakier hands.

Using the Technique With Generalized Anxiety

Because this technique can be done discreetly in any setting—as long as you simply keep your eyes downcast and not closed—it's a terrific tool for pulling the mind away from worry and directing it to the present moment. Again, the antithesis of worry is to be in the moment and not in the future or past. The next time you find yourself ruminating about a past mistake or fretting about the future, focus on the external world, noticing all the smells, sounds, and movement around you.

> *Because this technique can be done discreetly in any setting, it's a terrific tool for pulling the mind away from worry and directing it to the present moment.*

"You're gonna be fine," Stephanie said as she and Tisha approached the restaurant. She waved to their friends from college, who were seated at an outdoor table near the entrance. Tisha grabbed her elbow. "I don't think I can do this," she stammered, her heart pounding. She could feel her hands getting sticky with sweat. But Stephanie plowed forward, dragging Tisha behind.

"Hey Angie, Carleen!" Stephanie said as they walked up. She pulled out a chair for Tisha, who clumsily sat down, knocking her napkin and silverware onto the ground. Everyone laughed.

Focus inward, Tisha reminded herself, concentrating on her breath. Don't pay attention to their laughing. She inhaled evenly, noticing the way the air filled her lungs.

"You know what dropping a knife means, don't you?" Angie said. "It means you're gonna meet a man."

Stephanie laughed. "You're still as superstitious as you've ever been, aren't you, Angie?"

Angie didn't miss a beat. "And a spoon means meeting a woman. . . . I guess Tisha's hedging all her bets!"

Tisha picked up her napkin from the ground. She could feel her hands tremble as she placed it on her lap. Her heart raced. Focus outward, she told herself. She looked closely at the table—the glossiness of the wood, the clean white of the plates. A cherry tree a short way down the street was in full bloom, its fragrance filling the air.

"I'm so glad spring is finally here," Tisha managed to croak out. It was a complete non sequitur, but no one seemed to notice.

"Oh, I know," Angie said. "This winter was brutal." Stephanie and Carleen nodded in agreement, and lunch was on.

Just Relax! No, Really, Just *relax* . . .

OLIVIA RAN THROUGH the airport, her carry-on bag banging heavily against her hip. It was a miracle she'd gotten there at all, with the van driver's insistence on going slowly over the icy roads. Terminal C . . . Terminal C . . . Olivia scanned the signs overhead, searching for the direction to go.

It had been a rough semester. College classes were far more demanding than high school had been, and Olivia missed her old friends. Finals had been excruciating. She'd turned in her Texts and Contexts paper late, and she was sure she'd bombed her calculus exam. She hadn't slept more than a few hours in the past week, and last night she'd tossed and turned until 4 A.M. worrying about how she'd explain her abysmal grades to her parents. Now she was about to miss her flight.

Terminal C! Olivia raced down the wide hallway. The plane was boarding when she got there, a long line of people snaking out from the loading-bridge door. Olivia stopped and bent over, hands on her knees, trying to catch her breath.

NOW BOARDING ALL PASSENGERS FOR FLIGHT 4109 TO BALTIMORE, the overhead speaker announced. Olivia walked down the narrow loading bridge. She still felt dizzy from her sprint across the airport. On the plane, she found her seat and buckled her seatbelt. A toddler in the row behind her kicked the back of her seat while his mother tried to soothe his wailing baby sister. Snow was coming down hard outside the window. Olivia opened the air vent above her. She felt flushed and still out of breath. A heavy-set man in a gray suit took the seat next to her, struggling to get his briefcase into the carry-on space at his feet.

Suddenly Olivia felt everything close in around her. Her stomach clenched like she was about to vomit. Everything felt like it was spinning. Hands shaking, she tried to unbuckle her seatbelt. "Excuse me. . . . *Excuse* me!" she snapped as she frantically squeezed past the man in the gray suit.

A flight attendant approached her in the aisle. "Miss? Miss! You need to take your seat."

"I . . . I . . ." Olivia gasped, "I have to get off this plane!"

You've probably heard it a hundred times—friends or family members telling you, "Just relax!" Well, you'd relax if you could! No one enjoys experiencing the suffocating grip of panic, or the queasiness of social anxiety, or the constant tension of generalized anxiety.

Physical relaxation does not come naturally to people suffering anxiety. For people who suffer panic attacks, the mental tension of expecting an attack leads to tension in the body. For those with social anxiety, the fear of being humiliated can cause the body to tighten and be more vulnerable to panic or social anxiety symptoms. People with generalized anxiety may show tension-related arousal—headaches, TMJ, digestive problems, and so on—but not even notice how they have tightened up until they have pain somewhere.

People with any type of anxiety experience physical signs of that negative arousal. But you can take

People with any type of anxiety experience physical signs of that negative arousal. But you can take charge by intentionally relaxing your body.

charge by intentionally relaxing your body. And this, in turn, will lead to a more relaxed mind.

Assess Your Need to Relax

Panic, social anxiety, and generalized anxiety all have hallmark signs of tension or physical arousal. What physical indicators do *you* have? If you suffer from more than one kind of anxiety, you may check symptoms in more than one category.

Do You Have These Physical Symptoms?

Check off the symptoms you have in any of the following categories.

Symptoms of Panic

❏ Rapid heart rate
❏ Shallow breathing
❏ Digestive upset
❏ Sweating
❏ Shakiness, trembling
❏ Dizziness
❏ Exhaustion when the attack subsides
❏ Feelings of tingling or agitation long after the attack subsides

Symptoms of Social Anxiety

- ❏ Blushing
- ❏ Sweating
- ❏ Heart palpitations
- ❏ Shaking hands or knees
- ❏ Quivering voice
- ❏ Nausea

Symptoms of Generalized Anxiety

- ❏ Abdominal pain (this symptom is often reported by children)
- ❏ Chest pain
- ❏ Dry mouth or difficulty swallowing
- ❏ Headaches
- ❏ Muscle tension (neck, upper back, lower back)
- ❏ Holding your breath
- ❏ Muscle weakness
- ❏ Fatigue
- ❏ Trouble concentrating
- ❏ Restless sleep

All of these symptoms are related to your body's being in a state of arousal. Relaxation, done deliberately, can avert or alleviate these symptoms.

Progressive Muscle Relaxation

Progressive muscle relaxation is a first-line treatment for the physical tension of the anxious body. This technique not only eliminates tension-related stiffness and aches but also lowers arousal, which makes triggering anxious physical symptoms more difficult.

The muscle relaxation will take 10 to 15 minutes. The basic gist is to relax all muscle groups, one by one.

1. Make sure you're in a relaxed position, lying flat or sitting with your neck upright.
2. Close your eyes. Focus entirely on the sensations of each muscle group.
3. Add an image to the process. For example, imagine you are lying outside and the sun is gradually shining on you, hitting your toes first and then moving along your body as you go through this exercise.
4. If you're sitting up, begin at your head and move down. If you're lying down, begin at your feet and move up, working one group of muscles at a time.
   - Tense, hold, and then relax the muscle group. For example, curl your toes tight, tight, tight. Now release.

- Feel the warmth flood into them. With each exhalation of breath, feel the warmth flow into your toes.
- Repeat the tense, hold, and release three times. (It's amazing how much tension remains after just one or two tightenings.)

5. Go one by one through these muscle groups:
   - Scalp—raise your eyebrows to tighten the scalp.
   - Forehead—wrinkle your brow.
   - Face—squint your eyes, wrinkle your nose, and purse your mouth to tighten the face.
   - Neck—don't do neck circles, as they're hard on the spine. Try this instead:
     - Let your head drop forward with the weight pulling your chin toward your chest. You will feel the stretch down your back.
     - Return your head to a full upright position before leaning it back in the opposite direction.
     - Tilt your head to one side, with the ear moving directly toward the shoulder, and feel the stretch down your shoulder blade. When your head returns upright, feel the warmth flow in where the stretching was.
   - Shoulders—raise your shoulders up, hunching them, and then release the tension.

- Arms—tighten your forearm, wrist, and hand by clenching your fist.
- Back and abdomen—tighten this area by imagining a string pulling your belly button toward the spine and then release slowly.
- Buttocks—tighten by squeezing together.
- Thighs—tighten by tensing and releasing your quad muscles.
- Calves and shins—tighten by pointing your toes and feel the stretch down the shin and the contraction in the calf. Then reverse, by pulling the toe up and pushing the heel down. Feel the stretch down your calf and the contraction in the shin.
- Feet and toes—tighten by either curling the toes or pushing the foot into the earth.

6. With each muscle group, notice the warmth and then energy that suffuses the muscles as you release the tension. If you're using a specific image, such as the sun beginning to touch each part of you, think of that image as you go through each group.

7. If you did the exercise from the top down, end with an awareness of the soles of your feet feeling connected to the earth through the floor. If you did it from the bottom up, end with an awareness of feeling completely relaxed from head to toe.

8. Notice how totally relaxed, warm, and peaceful you are. Give yourself permission to remain relaxed as long as you want, or, if you're going on to another activity, give yourself permission to remain physically relaxed yet refreshed, alert, and fully present while doing it.

Physical tension is not going to disappear with just one session of relaxation. You need to learn over time to let go of tension on cue (see the next section). The best idea is to practice this every day until you feel you can let go of tension easily. Doing this at the same time every day is best, but bedtime gives the double advantage of preparing you to drift into sleep. Once you've gotten used to the exercise, you can use it to do the next technique—cued muscle relaxation.

Cued Muscle Relaxation

Cued muscle relaxation—where you cue physical relaxation by taking just one deep breath—is a fast, effective method that can be used no matter what type of anxiety you have. It's essentially a pairing of diaphragmatic breathing and progressive muscle relaxation. This is how you do it:

1. Several times a day, especially when you feel tense, take a deep diaphragmatic inhalation and recall the deep relaxation you felt when doing the progressive muscle relaxation exercise.

2. As you exhale, send negative energy out of your entire body and let relaxation flow in behind it. Use an image that represents letting tension go—such as plugging your feet into the earth or sending roots from your feet into the earth.

3. Accompany the slow, deep breath with a calming statement, such as "Now I am breathing in all that is of peace. Now I am breathing out all that is not of peace." Whether using an image or a phrase, draw peaceful relaxation inward as you inhale, and exhale the negative energy.

4. When you exhale, note how the muscles from your scalp to your toes are letting go of tension. Repeat this many times a day.

This technique allows you to cue muscle relaxation on demand, anywhere or anytime, without anyone noticing.

You can cue muscle relaxation on demand, anywhere or anytime, without anyone noticing.

Sphere of Light Imagery

There are many different imageries for relaxation, but the Sphere of Light works particularly well. It relaxes the whole body and takes less time than progressive muscle relaxation.

1. Imagine a sphere of light and energy above your head.
2. The light is a color you associate with peace, calm, healing, or energy. It's in abundant supply, so you can draw as much as you want into yourself.
3. As you inhale, breathe this beautiful energy and light in through the top of your head.
4. As you exhale, feel the flow of energy streaming through your scalp.
5. Repeat this with each of your body parts (face, head, neck, shoulders, arms, hands, fingers, torso, hips, buttocks, thighs, knees, shins, calves, ankles, feet, and toes). Breathe energy and light to each of the muscle groups as you inhale, and feel the energy flow through those muscles as you exhale.
6. Find a word that you associate with the sensation of total relaxation, such as "calm" or "peace," or even a sound such as "ah" or "mmm."

7. This energy provides a barrier to negativity for the day, preventing all criticism, disapproval, harsh words, or ill treatment from penetrating your heart. The barrier is permeable to all positive energy, so that words of praise, approval, and affection can immediately be received in the heart.

8. As the envelope of energy fades through the day, you can renew it with a deep breath, imagining the energy and light, and saying or hearing the relaxing sound or word you chose.

Exercise

You don't have to sit still to relieve your anxiety and tension. In fact, movement may be exactly what you need.

> *You don't have to sit still to relieve your anxiety and tension.*

A stunning amount of research demonstrates the many ways exercise is good for your mind and body. For the high-energy person with lots of muscle tension, physical activities are a better way of relaxing than sitting still is, but exercise can help people with all kinds of anxiety. Exercise:

- Promotes healthy brain activity by increasing blood flow
- Keeps the body healthy and able to respond effectively to stress
- Improves self-efficacy—a feeling often diminished when you are stressed

Getting Started

Vigorous aerobic exercise is best for anxiety because it's both a long-term relaxer and a short-term tension releaser. But starting at that pace may be too difficult. It's fine to build slowly, doing things you might actually enjoy, so that you have a good chance of staying with it.

Start small. You might begin by committing to walking the dog an extra 5 minutes, getting off the bus one stop before you have to, or walking around the block once whenever you check the mail. It's important to specifically decide on a small step and make a commitment to do it.

If you want to build up to 25–45 minutes of aerobic activity, start by asking yourself these questions:

1. What physical things do I like to do?
2. What are my opportunities to do them?
3. Is there anyone who would do them with me?

4. What is the largest possible step I can take in the direction of exercise? (Your goal should be to do a little more each week, until you have achieved the goal of 25–45 minutes of aerobic exercise at 70% of your maximum heart rate.)

5. How will I be accountable?

One way to be accountable is to use a simple chart. Draw seven columns, labeled with each day of the week. Every time you exercise, write down what type of exercise it was and how long you did it under the appropriate day. There are also smartphone apps that have good tracking options.

Stretch

Staying loose also helps with all kinds of anxiety. But never do anything that hurts! If it hurts, stop immediately.

Stretches can be done anywhere. Many of them can be practiced at work or school or while you're sitting in a car or airplane. Plus, they take relatively little time to do. You can do a stretch while thinking about the next question on a test, or while you wait for your computer to perform a function.

> *Stretches can be done at work or school or while you're sitting in a car or airplane.*

- *Arm stretch*. Simply yawn, stretch your arms upward, and release. Repeat.
- *Back stretch*. With your feet comfortably spread apart for support, let your torso fall forward, with your head gently leading the way down. Bend at the waist, and come back into an upright position by reversing the motion. Imagine that you are a puppet being released and then drawn upright by a string.
- *Overhead stretch*. Continue the back stretch into an overhead stretch once you are upright. Lift your arms, reaching high overhead, and lift your chin until you gaze directly up.
- *Leg lunges*. If you get up to walk somewhere, pause for a moment and try some gentle leg lunges.
- *Calf stretch*. If you have the opportunity to go up or down a few stairs, pause and, with your toes balanced on the edge of the stair step, let your heel drop. Do this for 2 seconds and then release. Repeat it a few times. You can do this one leg at a time with the other foot firmly planted on the step so you don't lose your balance.
- *Seated-at-your-desk head tilt*. You can do a simple head-tilt stretch while on the phone, looking at the computer, or reading, and not even lose time from work. Do not rotate your neck in a circle. Let your ear fall toward your shoul-

der as far as it can without hurting. Then raise your head upright. Now let your chin drop slowly to your chest, feel the stretch down your back, and raise your head upright again. Then drop the other ear toward the other shoulder and, again, raise your head. Finally, let your head feel heavy and drop slowly backward.

- *Seated-at-your-desk arm stretch.* Raise one arm straight overhead and then bend it at the elbow, reaching down and toward the other side of your body, as if you were going to scratch your other shoulder blade. Then relax. Take the same arm and reach across your chest and wrap your hand around the opposite shoulder. Using the unoccupied hand, grasp the elbow of the reaching arm and gently exert pressure to increase the stretch in the shoulder and upper arm.

- *Seated posture change.* Have a stool (or just a box) by your feet on which to rest them. For 15 minutes in each position, sit with one foot raised, then the other, then both, then neither. Put a back pillow or rolled towel behind your lower back, then your middle back, and then do without it.

Practicing these stretches will help keep you loose when work or life intervenes to make you uptight.

Slow Down

"I can't slow down!" you may say. "Why do you think I'm so stressed? I have too much to do!" This is a common refrain for the anxious person. But ask yourself this: How much better would you be at getting everything done if you weren't spending so much time being stressed?

The following activities are proven stress relievers, so you don't have to feel guilty about doing them!

- *Get a massage.* Several studies have shown that massage reduces stress and anxiety; relaxes muscles; aids in circulation, digestion, and excretion; and reduces pain perception. Being touched stimulates oxytocin, a hormone involved in feelings of being soothed and calm. Even the simplest massage from a family member may convey a feeling of being cared for and literally reduce the impact of stress.

- *Take a warm bath and use aromatherapy.* A warm bath also stimulates oxytocin and warmth relaxes muscles. Aromatherapy is the practice of using essential oils to enhance relaxation or target symptoms of tension and anxiety. The oils most consistently used for depression and anxiety are lavender, jasmine, ylang-ylang, sandalwood, bergamot, and rose. Several of these oils have been shown to have muscle-relaxant and sedative properties.

- *Stroll in the sun.* The skin should be protected from the UV rays of the sun, but our brains need the stimulation of light to develop good circadian rhythms (promoting sleep) and to prevent depressed and anxious states. Thirty minutes of walking outside provides enough light stimulation, and being in the warmth of the sun is also a good muscle relaxer.

- *Spend time near lapping or running water*—a lake, a river, an ocean—and breathe. The sounds are soothing, and the ionization of the air near bodies of water allows for greater relaxation.

Sleep!

It's impossible to be relaxed when you're exhausted. Good sleep underlies good health, including good mental health. The profound mental relaxation promoted by good rest is not obtainable in any other way.

Restless sleep or short nights due to overwork can make everything else about having anxiety harder. Here are some simple ways to improve the quality of your sleep:

- *Set a sleep schedule.* You'll find it easier to fall asleep, stay asleep, and wake up rested if you go to bed and wake up at the same time each day.
- *Make time for sleep.* Most adults need 7½ to 8 hours, adolescents need 9 to 10 hours, and children need more depending on their age.
- *Make the environment conducive to sleep.* The room should be as cool and dark as possible. Screen out noises, like people talking in another room or noise from the street. Turn off the television—white noise machines are better for blocking out sounds from the environment.
- *Make the anxious brain ready for sleep.* Keep caffeine use as low as possible, especially after noon. Eat well during the day and have a small high-carbohydrate snack before sleep. (This helps the brain use proteins and nutrients to regenerate itself.) Eliminate violent or exciting television for several hours before sleep. (This includes the news!) Avoid the computer several hours before sleep. (The light from the screen tells your brain to stay awake.) You can also try taking a warm bath and drinking herbal teas such as catnip or chamomile.

"Mom?" Olivia glanced nervously at her mother after they'd gotten in the car. "Thanks for driving all the way up here to get me. I'm . . . I'm really sorry."

Her mother gave her a tired smile. "It's okay, honey." She paused. "You know, I actually had pretty bad panic attacks myself when I was younger. I know how terrifying they are."

Olivia's eyes widened. "You did?" Her mother always seemed so in control.

"Mm-hmm. Before every exam—not very convenient!"

Olivia laughed. "What did you do?"

"Well, after almost failing a couple of classes, I finally found something that really worked. I'll teach it to you when we get home." She glanced at Olivia. "It takes some practice, but you have a whole month off before you have to fly back to school."

That month turned out to be a relaxing one. Olivia caught up on sleep, made an effort to get to the gym, and reconnected with her friends. She readily took to the progressive muscle relaxation her mother taught her, liking the way it made her feel even when she wasn't anxious.

The morning of her flight back to school, Olivia made a point of getting up early so she wouldn't feel rushed. At the airport, she did a few stretches before walking down the loading bridge. Everything was going fine—until she stepped on the plane itself. Just seeing the people packed into their seats and loading their baggage made her gut seize.

It's okay, she reminded herself. *Just breathe.*

She inhaled slowly. "I'm taking in everything that's calm," she said under her breath. She exhaled. "I'm pushing out everything else." She could feel her body loosen as she walked down the aisle. "I'm relaxed and taking in everything that's calm," she repeated, "and breathing out everything else."

By the time the plane took off, Olivia was looking out the window, wondering if she might be able to spot her mother's car headed home on the highway below.

Don't Make Mountains Out of Molehills

"You coming out for drinks tonight?" Stan clapped a big, warm hand on Todd's shoulder.

Todd looked up briefly from his computer screen. "I don't know. I've got a lot of this backlog to get through."

"Aw, come on!" Stan always seemed to be shouting, no matter what the conversation was. "You missed the last one, too!"

Todd tried to suppress his irritation. "I don't know, Stan. I'll try. . . . How late do you think y'all will be there?"

"Well, I don't know about the rest of 'em, but I'll be there as long as it takes to convince Hodges to pick me instead of Teddy for that promotion!" Stan gave a hearty laugh and lumbered down the hallway. "On second thought," he loudly added over his shoulder, "maybe you shouldn't come—I don't need the extra competition!"

A couple of hours later, Todd was sitting in his car outside O'Donnelly's Bar & Grill. Drinking with his coworkers was the last thing he wanted to do—just the thought of it exhausted him. But Stan was right. Showing up might help him get on Hodges's good side. He unbuckled his seatbelt, took a deep breath, and stepped out of the car.

Inside the bar, music blared and at least eight televisions, all set on sports stations, hung from the ceilings. Todd wished he were watching the game at home. He spotted his coworkers and headed toward them.

"Our boy Todd!" Stan bellowed, fanning his arm over the table with dramatic flair. "How nice of you to join us!"

Todd felt his stomach clench. Stan was already drunk, and Todd knew how awful he got when he'd had one too many. He dreaded being the butt of one of Stan's dumb jokes.

He looked for a seat. There were none. The waitress came over and asked for his order. Still standing, he blushed and nervously glanced around for a menu. He could feel himself begin to sweat. Everyone else could probably see it, too. Hodges could probably see it. Stan could definitely see it.

"Give him a Maker's Mark, on the rocks," Stan ordered. "Guy's had a long day. And get him a chair."

"I can get a chair," Todd stammered, his face reddening even more. Everyone was staring at him. He felt like an idiot—sweating and blushing like he was asking some girl to dance at a high school homecoming. Why had he even come out? This was going to be a disaster.

Thoughts that begin with the words "oh no!" are likely to be followed by the assumption that the worst will happen. Making a mountain out of a molehill—expecting things to be awful or terrible—is called "catastrophizing."

Catastrophizing is common in panic, social anxiety, and generalized anxiety. People who suffer panic or social anxiety tend to catastrophize both their symptoms and the outcome of their symptoms. They live in fear of having the strong negative feelings of a panic attack or of the possibility that they will blush, sweat, or shake in a social situation. People who have panic attacks often believe they are dying, going crazy, or losing control. And people with social anxiety are convinced that they'll be rejected or feel humiliated. When people with generalized anxiety feel that familiar sensation of dread coming on, they go into "scan mode" to see what could be causing it, usually assuming the sensation is due to more than just a glitch in their anxious brain.

When you suffer from anxiety, your body—for no good reason other than brain chemistry—generates sensations that feel like anxiety. And the emotional part of your brain, geared to protect you against bad things happening, reacts to these physical signals as if they are the truth. Convinced that if you're feeling physical symptoms of anxiety there must indeed be something very real to worry about, the emotional part of your brain catastrophizes the sensations. And it's hard to disbelieve your own brain telling you something bad is about to happen! That's why you need to deliberately identify and divert those thoughts.

> *It's hard to disbelieve your own brain telling you something bad is about to happen! That's why you need to deliberately identify and divert those thoughts.*

Assess Your Catastrophizing

Do *you* make mountains out of molehills? See if you recognize yourself in any of the following lists.

Catastrophic Thoughts

If you suffer panic, do you find yourself thinking that:

❏ Panicky physical sensations will always lead to a full-blown attack.

❏ You'll definitely panic in situations similar to ones in which you've previously panicked.

❏ You won't be able to handle panicky physical sensations or a panic attack.

❏ You might die, go crazy, or lose control.

If you suffer social anxiety, do you find yourself thinking that:

❏ You will always blush, stammer, and shake in social situations.

❏ Your significant other is bored, cheating, or needs a break from staying home with you.

❏ You will never be able to think of interesting things to say, or will inevitably embarrass yourself by saying the wrong thing.

❏ Others will reject you if they see your nervousness.

❏ Feeling humiliated is inevitable and you won't be able to get over it.

❏ Your contributions at work are not useful or needed by the team.

If you suffer generalized anxiety, do you find yourself thinking that:

❏ Common physical problems, like a rash or headache, are probably indicators of a major ailment like cancer—or that you might be seriously ill even in the absence of symptoms.

❏ Making a mistake at work will get you fired or demoted.

❏ Making a mistake in a friendship, like forgetting a lunch date, will cause people to dislike you or to tease you to show what a bad friend you are.

❏ Even though you know your worries sound crazy, they might be valid.

❏ If you are not careful enough, any accident that happens (like a child tripping and falling) or any negative event (like a water hose leaking in the laundry room) will be your fault.

❏ Common problems in relationships, like arguments, will ruin that relationship.

❑ You've probably forgotten something important, liking turning off the oven, and it will have disastrous consequences, like burning the house down.

Catastrophic thinking can take many forms—the previous lists identify just a few. I once had a client who lived on a small horse farm and was a competitive equestrian. Every time she had a less-than-perfect lesson with her riding instructor, she became distraught. "I'll never get this right!" she'd exclaim. "I should just sell the horses and move to town!" Another client, a young man with a new wife and baby, became paralyzed with fear that he'd installed a chandelier incorrectly, even though he'd done electrical work before. "I just worry that I made a mistake," he said, "and that the whole house is going to burn down, with my wife and daughter in it."

To defeat catastrophic thinking, you must use deliberate, emphatic logic to override the emotional voice telling you your symptoms are awful or a sign of something bad. In other words, you must use the conscious, logical part of your brain to override the unconscious, emotional part—to say, "Hey, wait a minute, brain! I know you think something very bad is happening, but

Say, "Hey, wait a minute, brain! I know you think something very bad is happening, but let's stop for a second to see if that's really true."

let's stop for a second to see if that's really true." The following methods will help you do just that.

Remember: A Feeling Is Just a Feeling

The belief that sensations of anxiety cannot be tolerated causes more trouble than the actual sensations themselves. Believing that you can't handle your anxiety not only intensifies the sensations, but also creates a sense of helplessness. And that helplessness interferes with taking control. A primary goal of managing anxiety is understanding that a pounding heart, a flushing face, or a sinking stomach are all just feelings—nothing more.

> *A primary goal of managing anxiety is understanding that a pounding heart, a flushing face, or a sinking stomach are all just* feelings— *nothing more.*

Panic Is Unpleasant—But Not Lethal

Are the physical symptoms of panic unpleasant? Absolutely. Unwelcome? Yes. Distracting? No doubt. But they are nothing more than that! They won't kill you. They are just sensations. Ask yourself: "Have I survived every panic attack?" (If you're reading this, the only answer is "yes"!)

If you suffer from panic, try this:

1. Identify the symptom that gets you on the catastrophic-thinking track (e.g., pounding heart or shortness of breath).

2. Write down the catastrophic thoughts you most often have and replace them with the corrective thought. For example, you might replace "if I panic it will be awful" with "panic is unpleasant—but it isn't lethal."

3. Use diaphragmatic breathing and distract yourself. For example, you might decide to look at pictures of your last vacation or pat your dog for a minute.

4. Evaluate how this worked. This step helps your brain fight the catastrophic thinking next time.

Coming to believe that "a feeling is just a feeling" requires paying attention to outcomes. Even a full-fledged panic attack is eventually going to stop and leave you unharmed. Noticing the outcome (that an attack was brief and you survived it) and that you suffer less when you don't catastrophize is vital to increasing your confidence that you can stop panic.

Embarrassment Is Just a Feeling

The flushing, trembling, sweaty feelings that social anxiety sufferers experience are very hard to control. Stopping the catastrophizing about these symptoms entails disputing what you believe will happen and then ignoring the physical sensations. Tell yourself, "Being noticed is not the same as being rejected." Of course, it's true that typical signs of embarrassment are obvious and that people can notice them if they're looking at you. What's *not* true is that others care about whether you're red or sweaty. It's not true that they will dislike you, reject you, or laugh at you (except if you're still in middle school).

Several women I've seen in my practice have used the strategy that one of my clients, Ingrid, used. In our first session, Ingrid preempted any discussion about her splotchy, flushed neck by saying, "You'll notice that my neck gets all red when I talk about things that I have feelings about, but don't worry about it. It doesn't mean anything. My mother and grandmother had that, too." She completely decatastrophized the splotchiness by telling me not to worry, and in that way she stopped herself from worrying about it as well.

Men seem to have more trouble announcing that these symptoms may happen before they actually do. When this is the case, they can minimize their distress by deciding they are going to ignore their symptoms if they happen. They can remind themselves that flushing, sweating, and shaking aren't the end of the world, and that they can use breathing to stay as calm as possible.

If you suffer from social anxiety, try this:

1. Identify your signs of embarrassment. Do you get red in the face, feel a bit nauseous, or find that your voice quivers?

2. Stop catastrophizing about this feeling. Note what you normally say to yourself—such as "it will be awful if they notice I'm sweating"—and replace that statement with "being noticed is not the same as being rejected."

3. Do diaphragmatic breathing and immediately distract yourself, perhaps by noticing all the decorations in the room.

4. Evaluate later: Did your feelings subside? Were you indeed rejected? Did you have some success in doing some of the social activity without symptoms?

Dread Is Just a Feeling That Can Occur Even When Nothing Is Wrong

People with generalized anxiety have a brain that's wired to look for trouble even when nothing is wrong. If you have generalized anxiety, you're familiar with that sinking feeling you sometimes inexplicably get—like before you leave for work in the morning, or when your son goes off to summer camp. Feeling the dread, your brain searches for something—anything—that might be wrong. "I must have made a mistake on the report I turned in yesterday," you may think. Or, "Johnny is probably going to get hurt hiking."

You can ward off these worried thoughts by declaring, "A feeling is just a feeling. It doesn't mean that something is wrong." Then distract yourself or shift to breathing or mindfulness.

"But what if something really *is* wrong and I ignore it?" you may ask. The important thing here is to ask yourself if the feeling *preceded* the need to look for something. If the answer is yes, then distracting yourself from the feeling is in order. "But," you might object, "what if I should be feeling dread about something that's about to happen and I ignore it?" I would answer that real trouble usually presents itself without equivocation. We get a document spelling it out, a blast from someone complaining about what we did (or didn't do), or some other very clear sign that we're in trouble. You can deal with the problem once you know it's an actual problem. Worrying ahead of time that Johnny might get hurt doesn't do any good. So shelve your worries until something actually happens—in the unlikely event that it does!—and then take appropriate action.

Of course, there are times when dread signals something we ought to pay attention to. In those cases your unconscious mind is noticing trouble and you physically feel it faster than your conscious brain can recognize it. If you have trouble figuring out whether the feeling stems from unfounded feelings or from something real, psychotherapy (or a trusted friend or two) can help. That said, people with anxiety are usually so overfocused on that physical "uh oh" feeling that they very rarely overlook signals of real trouble. It's therefore safe for anxiety sufferers to assume that their feeling of dread is just a brain glitch.

If you suffer from generalized anxiety, try this:

1. When you get that "uh oh" feeling, try to identify how you feel it in your body. Is it queasiness in your stomach? Tension in your back or jaw?

2. Stop catastrophizing about this feeling. Substitute a statement such as "dread is just a feeling that can occur even when nothing is wrong" or "if I really have a problem, I won't have to go looking for it."

3. Do diaphragmatic breathing and immediately distract yourself. Concentrate on whatever you're doing right at that moment, or turn on the radio, or start something that needs to be done, like unloading the dishwasher.

4. Evaluate later, noticing that the feeling went away and that no problem was causing it.

Debunk Thoughts About Dying, Going Crazy, or Losing Control

"I'm dying!" "I'm going crazy!" "I'm losing control!" Even after all my years of doing therapy, it never ceases to amaze me that these thoughts trouble nearly all panic sufferers. It would be great if it were as easy as just telling people they are not dying, going crazy, or losing control. The problem is that they already know that. The logical part of their brain is aware that they've gone through this many times and have not yet died, gone crazy, or lost control. But their emotional brain is still waiting for the catastrophe to happen. And the emotion is far too powerful and convincing to ignore.

I once had a client who had a panic attack relapse after many months of getting better at preventing them. Even though his logical brain was saying, "It's probably just panic," his emotional brain told him, "But *this* time it could be a heart attack." It was only after a visit to the emergency room and thousands of dollars for medical tests that his emotional brain finally believed his logical brain.

The following two steps will help you override your emotional brain:

1. Tell yourself you have always survived panic.
2. Watch how your breathing slows you down, and remind yourself that you know how to stop panic, even when it's uncomfortable.

Search and Ask

You can also debunk panicky thoughts by using what I call the "search and ask" method.

First, search for the exact image or thought you have when you panic. Get specific. What do you envision when you say to yourself, "I'm dying" or "I'm going crazy" or "I'm losing control"?

Then begin a process of asking, "What happens next?" until you can't go any further. This method is not intended to make you feel worse; the key is going through the thought to the other side.

Let's start by looking at the catastrophizing statement "I'm dying." Find an exact image of what you really fear—say, collapsing in the street. Now ask yourself, "What happens next?" Your answer might be, "They hook me up to machines" or "My chest hurts more" or "I'm blacking out." Keep on asking, "Then what happens?" until you get to "Then I die." Then, ask yourself again, "What happens next?" You aren't alone if you laugh when you realize that the panic would at least be over. But there's a good chance that exploring this ultimate fear will help you understand more about what your panic means to you.

For example, one of my clients, Dan, worried about losing his job and running out of money because he had no substantial savings. But his panic focused on fears of dying. I asked Dan when his fears were triggered and the answer was usually, "While I'm paying the bills." After I asked him to follow this with "What happens next?," he imagined that he had just barely managed to pay for everything when he would find an unexpected bill, and then he would panic because there was no extra cash, and then he would have a heart attack, and then he would be taken to the hospital where he would be attended to by a host of emergency room people who could not save him. Then he laughed when he realized that he was more bothered by the idea that people failed in their duty to save him than by the idea of dying! And then he said, "If I had extra cash, I would never panic."

By pursuing his thoughts all the way through dying, Dan was able to see that what he really feared was his financial challenge. The catastrophic thought "I am dying" was just a distraction from addressing his real problem. Once we knew his real problem, we could talk about ways of dealing with it.

Now let's look at the catastrophizing statement "I'm losing control!" If you fear losing control, ask yourself, "If someone were observing me, what exactly would I look like? What would I be doing or saying?" Describe your behavior, not your feelings. Every time you describe one action, keep asking the question, "Then what?"—all the way through to the end of the panic attack. For example, a mother who won't go on a field trip with her daughter because she fears panicking on the bus might imagine herself short of breath, looking wild-eyed. When she asks herself, "Then what?" she might respond with "I would run off the bus!"—as if that's proof of losing control. When asked the question "Then what?" again, she might feel confused, wondering, "Isn't that enough?" But, pondering it further, she might find a way to get back on the bus or come to the realization that the other parents can manage the field trip without her. By using this question again and again to walk yourself through to the end of the attack, you may recognize that your fear of losing control is invalid.

Finally, let's look at the catastrophizing statement "I'm going crazy!" Of all the fears, this one is least likely to have a vivid realistic image. Usually people are only aware that some part of them is afraid that panic means they are crazy. But visualizing a specific image helps here, too. Ask yourself, "What does going crazy look like?" Run through the image like a movie, pursuing it until the panic is ended. When you know what underlies the fear of being crazy, you'll know how to resolve that fear and you'll be less likely to catastrophize.

Is This Like Any Other Experience You've Seen?

Remembering a real experience allows you to logically compare your panic to the feared catastrophe. One client of mine, Norman, worried that he was going crazy every time he had a panic attack. When I asked him to identify a specific image of going crazy, he said, "I'd be pacing around and waving my arms in the air." I then asked him what other experiences his panic attacks were like. He replied that they reminded him of his uncle, who was schizophrenic and had lived with Norman's family when Norman was young. The uncle was often irrational and paced a lot, and on more than one occasion he had been removed from the house when he "went crazy." This was scary to young Norman. By talking through the image of going crazy, Norman realized he was not his uncle, and his fear of going crazy disappeared.

When the Catastrophic Fear Is Rooted in Trauma

Some catastrophic fears are rooted in a past traumatic experience, and a trigger in the environment or in relationships can set these fears in motion without your even being aware of it, especially if the trauma was in childhood. When this is the case, identifying the trigger is an important part of debunking your fears of dying, losing control, or going crazy.

In some cases, though, discovering the trigger may not be enough. If you have a history of trauma, it may be best to explore its impact in psychotherapy. A therapist can help you better understand what happened, and how you can move beyond it.

Plan to Panic

What?! Isn't the point of this whole book to help you *avoid* panic? Why would you actually plan to *panic*?

Planning to panic may seem counterintuitive, but it's a great way to stop catastrophizing about the possibility that you will panic. One of the biggest problems with panic is that its triggers tend to grow. For example, if you once panicked while you were driving on the highway in the rain, you're probably afraid of panicking the next time you drive on the highway in the rain. That becomes a trigger. But then the trigger grows. You may start to fear driving on *any* street in the rain. And then you may start fearing driving completely, even on nice days. And then you may fear that you're going to panic whenever it rains, even if you're not driving. Your fear mushrooms, becoming bigger and bigger.

It's unlikely that you'll be able to avoid every potential panic trigger. So just plan on panicking! Planning to panic involves eight simple steps. Check them off as you complete them.

___ 1. Learn to breathe away panic (Anxiety Buster 2).

___ 2. Review each aspect of the situation you've been avoiding (e.g., highways, driving, rain).

___ 3. Next, imagine yourself in the situation. Note every aspect of the situation that caused you to feel nervous, and apply a method to calm down (such as Sphere of Light imagery, from Anxiety Buster 4) while you imagine it.

___ 4. Now practice a real-life mini version of the situation or activity. For example, plan to get on a short stretch of road at a time when it's not too busy. Take a friend who can take over driving if you do start to panic. Stop the practice session at the planned end time, even if it's going well.

___ 5. Write down exactly what you will do if or when you panic in the future. Carry your plan with you on an index card or in your smartphone.

___ 6. Review your plan before you go into the situation, and have it handy so you can grab it if you panic.

___ 7. Then try it for real, knowing that if you panic, you have a plan.

___ 8. Evaluate how it went:

- Commend yourself for handling difficulties.
- Praise yourself for entering the situation without panic.
- Decide how to amend your plan if you had a problem.
- Notice that you lived through it no matter how it went.

"I DOUBT HODGES NOTICED anything," Todd's sister, Paula, said as she served them both another helping of lasagna. "You're too sensitive."

"I looked ridiculous!" Todd argued. "You weren't there. You should've seen how they were all staring at me."

Paula shook her head. "They were looking at you because you'd just gotten there! They were probably wondering how to get you a chair."

"And Stan!" Todd clearly wasn't going to drop the subject. "It was like he was *trying* to embarrass me! Like I couldn't find my own chair or order a drink."

It dawned on Paula that she needed to try a different approach. "Okay, okay. So they were all staring at you. So what? So what if you were sweating? Lots of guys sweat."

Todd was suddenly silent, looking at her.

"And who cares if Stan was acting like he always does, trying to control everything?"

"Yeah, but in front of Hodges . . ." Todd protested, a little less emphatically.

"Stan always makes everyone uncomfortable, Todd. I'm sure Hodges has seen that a million times."

Todd considered this. Paula had a point. "Well, that

might be true . . . but I hate how I always turn bright red—no one else does that."

"Okay, so you're the only one at work whose face flushes. Who cares? It's not the end of the world."

Todd took another bite of lasagna.

"Look," Paula continued, "the next time you go out with those guys, just ignore the sweating and the red face and all the rest of it." She flashed him a smile. "And figure out what you're gonna drink at least a hundred yards before you reach Stan."

That last piece of advice had been a joke, but Todd took the suggestion anyway at the next office get-together, ordering a beer at the bar before looking around for his coworkers. As he approached their table, he could see that Stan was drunk again, spouting off about some inane thing at the top of his lungs. "Oh, God—here we go again," Todd thought, "I know he's gonna try to mess with me." But then he stopped himself. Paula's pep talk had been a good one. Who cared if he ended up the target of Stan's dumb jokes? He reminded himself that it wasn't that big a deal in the grand scheme of things.

As he sat down, Todd noticed that Hodges's assistant was looking at him. She was probably wondering why he'd bothered to come, after the fiasco of last week's night out.

Then she got up and moved her chair beside Todd's. "Thank heavens you're here," she whispered, leaning toward him and squeezing his arm. "Someone to save me from having to listen to that racket."

Todd blushed. But this time he didn't mind.

Stop and Swap

MOONLIGHT SHONE THROUGH the bedroom window, throwing shadows of trees on the wall. Carrie glanced at the clock: 1:52 A.M. Eric slept soundly next to her. He made it look so easy! Carrie got up to close the curtains, but it didn't help. 2:13 A.M. She pulled the covers up under her chin and forced her eyes closed. She'd had a sinking feeling all day, a sense that something was wrong. But what?

Carrie scanned through the day in her head. Had she forgotten to send her course proposal to the department head? No, she could remember composing the e-mail to him. . . . Wait! Had she forgotten to include the attachment at the end? Carrie climbed out of bed and went downstairs to check her laptop. She scrolled through the sent messages until she found the e-mail and clicked on it. There was the attachment, safe and sound. Carrie sighed and went into the kitchen to get a glass of water. Maybe it was Avery. He'd barely eaten that morning before school. What if he was sick?

She went back upstairs and quietly opened Avery's bedroom door. She gently felt his forehead with the back of her hand. He didn't feel hot. Could something psychological be making him nauseous? She'd overheard some mothers at the playground talking about bullying a few days ago. What if Avery was getting bullied? Carrie closed his door and went back to her bedroom. 2:28 A.M.

Lying in bed, she stared at the ceiling. That had to be it. Avery hadn't said that he had an upset stomach, but why else wouldn't he have eaten? Suddenly Carrie remembered that his friend Adam was having a birthday party soon. Why hadn't his mother called to invite Avery? Carrie nudged Eric awake.

"Honey, do you think everything's okay with Avery?"

Eric mumbled something inaudible.

"It's just that he didn't eat much breakfast this morning, and I just realized he wasn't invited to Adam's birthday party."

"Huh?" Eric tried to shake off his grogginess.

"Adam's birthday party," Carrie repeated. "Avery is being excluded."

"Oh, sorry." Eric yawned. "I forgot to tell you. Lynn called yesterday. Adam's party is this Saturday . . . at noon, I think." Eric rolled onto his side and put his pillow over his head.

How could Eric have forgotten to mention this? What if Avery had missed the party all because Eric hadn't passed on the message? Didn't he care enough to remember something that important?

Actually, now that she thought about it, Eric *had* seemed disengaged at home lately. He'd forgotten to bring the camera to Avery's Little League game last weekend, and he seemed to be spending longer hours at work.

"Honey?" Carrie nudged Eric again. He grunted. "Is everything okay with . . . with us?"

Eric turned over to face his wife. "What? Carrie, of course everything's fine with us." He squinted at the clock: 2:56 A.M. "And it'll be even more fine if you let me get some sleep."

Ambiguity causes anxiety. When you don't know what's happening or might happen, or what to do about what's happening, you start to feel anxious. And in an attempt to get rid of that anxiety, you go into "what if" thinking mode. "What if I made a mistake at work?" "What if my son is sick?" "What if my husband is thinking of leaving me?"

"What if" thinking is a reasonable response to normal anxiety about something that's ambiguous. If you're able to figure out what is going on, you can resolve the ambiguity and take action. For example, suppose you're feeling anxious about starting college. Your "what if" thoughts might be: "What if I can't make friends? What if I can't handle the workload?" These "what if" thoughts are helpful, because there are ways you can address them. You can look into extracurricular groups that will help you make friends, and you can go through the course catalog to select courses that will give you a balanced workload.

But people with anxiety disorders have a brain that's primed to feel anxiety even when absolutely nothing is wrong. And that's when those "what if" thoughts begin to cause trouble. Because there is no real problem, you start creating unreasonable "what if" scenarios.

People with anxiety disorders have a brain that's primed to feel anxiety even when absolutely nothing is wrong.

"What if I lose my job and can't support my family?" "What if my wife dies in a car accident?" These thoughts are your brain's effort to get rid of unpleasant anxiety, but if there's no real risk of losing your job, and if your wife is not in imminent danger of dying in a car accident, then the "what if" thinking does not resolve the anxiety.

In fact, it makes it worse! Because now your thoughts are crowded with potential problems that only might be issues. Your anxiety gets worse because the "what if" thinking has created real ambiguity. You feel bad, you don't know why, and you can't figure it out. This is how "what if" thinking spirals into a vicious circle.

Of course, when your "what if" thoughts aren't connected to any real-life situation, you eventually realize they were wrong. You finished another day at work without getting a pink slip. Your wife got home (again) without having a car accident. Realizing this, you feel somewhat better. But then, because your brain is primed to be anxious without a real-life cause, you start to feel the anxiety all over again, and you begin another cycle of "what if" thinking. As soon as one worry is resolved, another pops up in its place.

Assess Your "What If" Thinking

Anxious thoughts can be very convincing, even when they aren't connected to any real-life problem.

Are You Plagued by "What If" Thoughts?

Check off the statements that describe you.

❏ I'm constantly wondering if I've bothered people at home or work.

❏ I often wonder if physical sensations I have could be signs of a disease.

❏ I spend time researching symptoms on the Internet to reassure myself that I'm not sick.

❏ I review my work and my calendar repeatedly to see whether I've forgotten or missed something important.

❏ I spend hours or days feeling anxious, as if something bad is about to happen. (I wait for the other shoe to drop.)

❏ When someone tells me that he or she wants to talk, I immediately assume I will be chastised, fired, or told I have done something wrong.

❏ I have often gotten rid of one anxious thought only to have another pop up with the same intensity.

If you make a mistake, no matter how small, do any of these apply to you?

❏ I think over and over about what bad things can happen when I make a mistake.

❏ If I make a mistake at work, I spend hours worrying if I will get into serious trouble, even if I'm not sure anyone has noticed it.

❏ If I suspect I've made a social error, such as forgetting a name, dropping food on someone's carpet, or laughing when someone was being serious, I think that friends will talk about me or stop liking me. I can feel sick for days about it.

❏ I have anxious thoughts for days or even weeks prior to an activity during which I might have a panic or social anxiety attack.

❏ I think about mistakes I made in the past and wonder if I could still get into trouble now.

If you checked any of the boxes in these two lists, the Stop and Swap technique will help you. If you checked three or more boxes, it means that anxious thoughts are interfering with your life and you might need all the interventions that go with Stop and Swap.

Stop and Swap

There are two important components of the Stop and Swap method. One is telling yourself "stop!" every time you have a negative, anxious thought. The other is swapping that negative thought for a thought or activity that's positive or productive.

But first it's important to recognize the tricks that anxiety plays on you. Anxious thoughts can be very convincing, but you need to learn to tell yourself: My anxious thoughts are not true or valid.

> *Tell yourself: My anxious thoughts are not true or valid.*

"But what if I really *am* about to get fired?" you ask. "What if my anxiety isn't tricking me this time?" The key here is to check whether the anxiety is about something that's happening now or about something that *might* happen. Did your boss just put you on probation? If he did, then your anxious thoughts are perfectly reasonable! But if there's no clear, real-life evidence that something is wrong right now, you can assume that your anxiety is just getting the better of you.

If you have trouble telling yourself that your anxious thoughts aren't true, spend some time figuring out why you might think your anxious thought is useful—and then challenge that assumption until you're clear that the thought is worthless to you. For example, suppose you're worried that your husband is planning on leaving you—despite no evidence that he's dissatisfied with the relationship—and no matter how hard you try, you can't shake these thoughts. Ask yourself, "Why might I think this anxious thought is useful?" Perhaps it's because it makes you feel like you'll be more prepared for the bad news if or when it comes. Now challenge that assumption. Will you be any less able to pack your belongings and find a new place to live if you *haven't* been worrying that he's going to leave you? Will you be any less devastated about the breakup? No! In fact, your constant worrying might even be taking a toll on him and making the situation worse. Your anxious thoughts are worthless to you.

"Self, Stop!"

Whenever you notice an anxious thought popping up, tell yourself firmly: "Self, stop!" Interrupt the negativity as quickly as you can, and do it every time you have a negative thought.

Why does this work? It has to do with how our brain functions. Any thought we think repeatedly—whether it's positive or negative—makes a sort of neurobiological rut in our brain. And once that rut is set, we become more and more likely to think in that way. That's a problem when the thoughts are negative, anxious ones.

Think of it like sledding down a snowy hill. There's one track that leads safely to the bottom of the hill, and another that veers off into the bushes. The more times your sled ends up going down the negative track into the bushes, the more entrenched that track gets, and the more likely you are to find yourself in the bushes again.

Telling yourself "Stop!" is like putting a shovelful of snow in that negative track and forcing the brain down a more positive one. Your brain/sled may still try to veer off the positive track, but the more times you can block the negative one, the more likely you'll be to get to the bottom of the hill safely.

But that's just half of the solution—and it won't work without the second half. Read on!

Swap It Out

Blocking a negative thought means you'll be less likely to have that thought in the future. But—and this is a big but—the thought will bounce right back if you have nothing to replace it with. You have to swap the thought out for something better.

So what do you swap it out with?

> Blocking a negative thought means you'll be less likely to have that thought in the future. But you also have to swap the thought out for something better.

- Think of an affirmative statement that challenges the negative one.
- Pick a pleasant or productive thought to focus on for the day. Maybe it's remembering a fun, recent outing to the park with your grandchildren, or deciding what restaurant you'd like to eat at this weekend.
- Sing! Yes, singing is a great choice because your whole brain gets busy when you sing.
- Listen to music or an audio book.
- Recite an inspirational verse or mantra.
- Return your attention to the work you are doing, taking care to remain in the here and now.

What does this look like in practice? One of my clients, Preston, was plagued by worries about his health. His annual physical had gone fine, but Preston was still skeptical. What if he had an illness that wasn't detectable by regular tests? Logically, Preston knew his worries were unfounded, but his anxiety persisted. So he applied Stop and Swap. Every time an anxious thought about his health popped up, Preston said, "Stop!" and then replaced the thought with: "I'm good at noticing things. If I have symptoms of a true illness, I'll spot them." He then distracted himself by looking at the wallpaper he'd put on his smartphone—a photo of himself playing volleyball at his last family reunion.

Find Your Type of "What If" Thinking

Stop and Swap works well with all kinds of anxious thoughts. But different types of "what if" thinking present different kinds of challenges. What kinds of "what if" thoughts do *you* tend to have? Find them here and then apply the techniques for that type.

Rumination With a Theme

To ruminate means to think something over and over, like a cow chews cud, even though nothing about the thought changes when you do. You chew on an idea without resolving it or solving it.

Sometimes ruminative thinkers get stuck on specific topics, such as whether they've offended someone, have made mistakes at work, have a disease, or have failed to notice some important detail. People who ruminate with a theme tend to be okay when not reminded of their problem, but they also believe that if they could just resolve this one situation, they wouldn't be anxious again. Sadly, that is rarely true. They may get a brief spell of relief, but then some other "what if" thought will arrive.

If your ruminations have a theme, there is an additional vital step to insert in the Stop and Swap method. You must identify whether your worried thought relates to a previous life experience.

For example, if you had a parent with a chronic illness, you might be hyperalert to signs of that illness in yourself. Recognizing that your worries about your health are connected to this past experience will help you challenge the negative thought—perhaps with something like, "Dad had diabetes, but I'm careful to eat right and exercise, and my last medical checkup was fine."

Or perhaps your parents were neglectful of you when you were a child, and now you ruminate on thoughts about making a parenting mistake with your own child. Your negative-thought replacement might be: "I have been a caring and involved parent so far, and I will continue to be. I can break the pattern."

Thoughts of the Home or Workplace in Danger

This is basically the "Did I leave the oven on?" scenario, which is a type of "what if" thinking. There are many variations: "Did I turn off the coffee pot/lights/curling iron?" "Did I lock the doors?" "Did I close the windows?" "Did I blow out the candle?" "Did I bring in the dog?"

This type of thinking is often the result of inattentiveness due to the preoccupied, anxious mind. These types of worriers do not stay in the here and now. Instead, they rush ahead with thoughts like, "What if traffic is bad this morning?" or "How will I get all my work done today?" or "How did I not notice how late it is?" Distracted by these thoughts, these worriers fail to pay attention to what they are doing in the present. As they leave work or home, they perform the tasks of leaving for the day on autopilot—and once they're on the road, the "what if" thinking strikes.

There is one really good fix for this kind of anxiety. Pay attention out loud—especially when you are already rushed and anxious. Whenever you leave your home or your workplace, recite aloud the things you're doing. "I am turning off the oven. I am getting my wallet. I am turning out the lights. I am locking the door." Saying it aloud helps you mentally slow down and concentrate. It also helps you remember what you've done after you're on the road.

Hypochondria-Like Thoughts

Hypochondria is fearing that some benign physical symptom is a sign of a serious disease. Every headache turns into a brain tumor, every sore throat is cancer, every little skin rash becomes a flesh-eating bacteria.

This kind of "what if" thinking gets even more problematic when you begin researching your symptoms on the Internet.

You either waste a lot of time or really scare yourself when you find all the possibilities for what your symptoms could mean. Watching television can also exacerbate the problem. Commercial breaks are full of advertisements for drugs that treat countless conditions you've never even heard of, and news programs often feature stories about diseases you might catch or your risk of exposure to contaminants. Soon, every little sniffle or pain seems dangerous.

You can deal with these worries by following these steps:

1. Get it out in the open. Sometimes hearing your fear aloud makes it seem ridiculous.

2. Do not go on the Internet to research. If a condition is serious at this moment, you will have indisputable indicators: significant pain, a high fever, out-of-control vomiting, bleeding, fainting, and so on. These are physical signs that cannot be ignored—indications that you should seek help right now. You don't need to research them.

3. For lesser symptoms that trouble you because they might be something, ask yourself, "What would be the sign that this symptom is important?" This would include any sign that the condition is worsening. For example, a rash might spread or become painful or a fever might persist. You might need to ask someone for input while you get better at this.

4. Decide when you will evaluate your symptoms again. For example, you might decide to check on your rash in 3 hours, and if it's still the same, you'll check it again 24 hours later. Do not keep checking beyond that.

5. Do not seek reassurance from others—rather, seek information. For example, "I am worried about whether I should take medicine for my allergies. I heard it can be hard on my heart and I don't know if that's true." Identify one knowledgeable person you could ask about that.

6. Then do Stop and Swap as described earlier.

Rumination About Too Much to Do

There are times in life when responsibilities are truly burdensome. Maybe you're working and also going to school, or maybe you're a working single parent. However, people who have difficulty prioritizing, planning, or following through may feel overwhelmed even without an exceptional burden of work.

One of my clients, Brock, felt that he had fallen apart since starting an internship at school. He was expected to quickly learn all the tasks the job entailed and deal with the people at the job site. At the same time, he had a pile of journals to read for his internship seminar class. He felt panicky and was plagued by "What if I fail?" thinking. To deal with his stress, he began playing video games—often for hours at a time. This did provide a distraction and give him some relief, but it certainly didn't solve his problem of having too much to do! Brock needed a plan to get his work done. He needed to prioritize his tasks. And he needed to get started.

Make a Plan

Learning how to plan and prioritize is the best solution to this kind of unproductive thinking. Anxiety Buster 7, Contain Your Worry, goes into detail about planning. I only mention it here because it's common for ruminators to review a situation over and over without deciding how they will handle it. Once you make a plan, follow it! Don't revise it over and over—that's just "what if" thinking in disguise.

Do the Worst First

This one little method works wonders. Do whatever you're dreading right away and get it over with. Maybe it's making a phone call you don't want to make. Instead of spending all day feeling anxious about making the call, just do it first thing and get it out of the way. What a relief!

> *Do whatever you're dreading right away and get it over with.*

Make a List With Time Frames

Parents, people who work two jobs, people who work and go to school—all face a multitude of tasks that may seem like too much to do. If this applies to you, create a list with time frames to keep your expectations of yourself reasonable. False expectations about how much you can do will make you anxious, and this kind of list is the best remedy.

Begin by accurately estimating how long (in minutes) each thing will take. Then figure out what items are most important. When you can identify how much is possible for you to get done in a day, you can have accurate expectations about your day. You may be skeptical, but there is power in this kind of list: It makes you face reality. If you can't get a task done, then you can't get it done.

If your list is far longer than can be accomplished in a single day, try the following adjustments:

1. Remove items with later deadlines. Keep a separate list for those.
2. If you see that you're not going to be able to complete something on the list and you react by saying, "Oh, no! I have to get that done today!" then change your priorities to accommodate what's most pressing. You may have to face the reality that you're going to miss a deadline. That may

involve asking others for an extension or telling someone you won't be able to complete an expected task. It can be a great relief to admit you're not going to get something done and set a new, more reasonable deadline.

3. Don't focus on what you can't get done. Just focus on what you will get done and feel good about it.

Move!

Stop and Swap is about helping the stuck brain move into more productive thinking. But moving your body can help move your brain, too—especially if you have panic or social anxiety. And if you couple the movement with a thought replacement, so much the better. Here are some ideas for moving your body:

- Do something around the house, especially if you've been sitting at the computer or television. Put in a load of laundry, wash a dish, walk the dog, tidy up a room.
- At work, take a walk down the hall, go to the water fountain, or walk up and down steps in a stairwell for a minute while thinking about the work task you will do when you get back to your work station.
- Stretch. If you're standing in a checkout line or waiting for

the bus to arrive, do a few simple arm stretches. If you're driving, you can do a couple of side-to-side neck stretches without taking your eyes off the road. (Reread Anxiety Buster 4 for more on stretches.)

Plan Ahead and Be Persistent

Decide on a thought replacement *before* you find yourself in the grip of worry. Don't wait until you're stuck in the middle of a rumination to figure out what to think about instead.

Go ahead and do it now. Put the book down for a moment and think about how you want to swap out your worried thought. Should it be with a positive thought that challenges the negative one, such as, "I've successfully dealt with problems in the past, and I'll be able to deal with future ones, too"? Should it be with a recitation of a song lyric or scripture passage? If so, pick one. Should it be with a photograph of your grandkids? Find the photograph and put it in an accessible place on your computer desktop or phone, or print it out and put it in your wallet, where you can quickly find it.

Then, be persistent! Carving new, positive pathways in your brain won't happen overnight. You may even find that your anxious thoughts actually increase briefly when you start practicing Stop and Swap. But you can take comfort in the knowledge that every time you do this method, you're making it a little bit easier to do the next time. And even a spike in anxious thoughts will eventually be followed by a rapid decrease. Be patient!

You can take comfort in the knowledge that every time you do this method, you're making it a little bit easier to do the next time.

STOP AND SWAP worked well for Carrie. Although her ruminations didn't seem to have a consistent theme, some soul-searching about what her anxious thoughts might be related to eventually led to a revelation. Carrie's childhood home life had been stable—until she was 9 years old, when her father was diagnosed with cancer. He was started on an aggressive regimen of chemotherapy that left him too weak to continue working at the construction company that employed him. Eventually the cancer went into remission, but the illness had taken its toll. Still out of work and depressed, Carrie's father began drinking heavily. And when he drank, things got ugly.

One afternoon, Carrie's mother picked her up from school with the car packed full of their belongings. Carrie never saw her father again. She and her mother spent the next two years shuttling between bleak apartments and homeless shelters.

By the time Carrie was in high school, her mother had gotten a job as an administrative assistant and they lived in a nice little cottage on the edge of town. Carrie studied hard and excelled in school, winning a scholarship to a prestigious university. She was the first in her family to go to college. But despite her academic success, the sense that everything could suddenly come apart stayed with her, fueling her anxiety.

Disciplined by nature, Carrie didn't have much trouble saying "Stop!" every time a worried thought popped up. In fact, she tackled this part of the technique with the same intense energy that she normally used on ruminating. But swapping the negative thoughts was more difficult, because her brain was so good at imagining a wide variety of possible problems. Every time she managed to tamp one down, a completely different one would erupt. Finally she settled on humming her favorite song—Sam Cooke's "A Change Is Gonna Come"—and reciting the mantra "I'll deal with the problem, whatever it is, after it actually materializes. Until then, I'll go with the flow." That statement was general enough that she could apply it to practically everything: "I'll deal with Avery's problems with friends after he actually comes home crying or has behavioral issues. I'll talk with Eric about our marriage after he's actually said he's unhappy."

But Avery didn't come home crying, and Eric never said he was unhappy. In fact, after Carrie got her worry under control, the family seemed more stable than ever.

Contain Your Worry

"DAD!" RACHEL SAID, exasperated. "You've got to stop this! Everything's going to be fine."

Adam sighed and looked at his daughter. Nine months pregnant, she was about to be the mother of his first grandchild. "I just don't see why I can't meet with your doctor," he said.

"Because he's a busy man, and he's already spent a huge amount of time with Eli and me—that's why. We already know everything we need to know." Rachel pointed at the paint roller sitting in the tray. "Now hand me the roller and let's get this thing done." Half of the nursery was now yellow, the same color Rachel's room had been when she was a child. Adam wished Beth were still alive to see it. She would've been happy to know their daughter was carrying on the tradition.

He handed the roller to Rachel. "Well, I wish you'd just get a C-section. What if he's on vacation when you go into labor?"

"Dad, we already discussed this." Rachel began rolling the paint on the wall as Adam finished taping off the windowsill. "St. Vincent's is the best hospital in the city. You don't need to worry."

"Even good hospitals can have a bad doctor, Rachel."

Rachel ignored the comment and continued painting. A reggae song came on the radio, filling the silence between them. Adam wished it could drown out the thoughts in his head as well. What if something went wrong during the delivery? Or worse, what if something was wrong with the baby?

"Is it too late now to get an amnio?" he asked.

"We're not getting an amnio, Dad."

Adam pushed down a piece of tape that had come up at the corner. He glanced at Rachel. "Your mother would have wanted you to get the amnio," he said, quietly.

Rachel slammed down the paint roller angrily. "Look," she said, turning to face her father. "I asked you to come over to help paint so that we could do something special together. It's supposed to be fun. Just you and me getting the baby's room ready, together." She switched off the radio and brushed a stray hair from her forehead, leaving a smear of paint in its place. "And now . . . now you're ruining it."

Everybody worries, but people with generalized anxiety elevate worry to an art form. They take normal worries and make them into monstrous impediments to clear thinking, blowing everything out of proportion.

You may even be aware of the fact that your worries have become excessive, and wonder whether you're going crazy. Your logical brain knows the things you worry about are unlikely to happen, but in your gut you feel as if they could.

The intensity of these kinds of worries is due to the highly active brain commonly seen in people with generalized anxiety. That active brain actively worries. But your active brain can help you, too—giving you the energy to remain persistent in controlling your worry.

Worry is insistent. It feels important. But when you persistently work against it, worry abates. That's the goal of this Anxiety Buster—to get worry back down to normal proportions.

> *Worry is insistent. It feels important. But when you persistently work against it, worry abates.*

Assess Your Worry

Out-of-control worry isn't just a nuisance—it can negatively affect your entire life. It can interfere with everyday functioning and rob you of the pleasure you once felt in doing things you enjoy.

Do You Need to Contain Your Worry?

Check off the statements that describe you:

- ❏ My worry is hard to control; it creeps into my thoughts all day.
- ❏ I'm so preoccupied with my worries that I rarely feel joy anymore.
- ❏ I can't pay attention. My worry interferes with attention for the details that enrich or inform life.

Total number of boxes checked: _____

- ❏ I spend a lot of time feeling concerned about the outcome of projects I undertake at home or work.
- ❏ I worry that every fever and cough my child has is going to escalate into a life-threatening illness.

❏ Whenever I hear about a potential health risk from a food (such as artery-clogging saturated fats), I immediately stop eating it and get it out of the house.

❏ I've worried about whether I've fed guests food that might cause food poisoning.

❏ I've worried that I will be put in jail for mistakes on income tax forms or failure to comply with some detail that has legal repercussions.

❏ I've had serious concerns about becoming homeless, even though I'm well educated and have a good job that I'm not currently in danger of losing.

❏ I cope quite well with real, even disastrous, problems.

Total number of boxes checked: _____

If you checked one of the boxes in the first list, you'll want to use the methods presented here. If you checked two or more boxes in the second list, pay special attention to all these methods and seriously consider getting additional support in your effort to be persistent about containing your worry.

When you're no longer able to shrug off worry, it's time to take charge and learn how to manage it. No one can completely avoid worry all the time, but anyone can contain it.

Get the Right Reassurance

Do you try to calm down by getting reassurance from someone else? Do you ask people to tell you that what you're worried about can't happen? You may believe you won't worry anymore if you can just get the right solution or the right information, and this leads you to ask other people for reassurance.

But have you noticed that just when you're starting to feel reassured, another worry pops up and you start the cycle all over again? Maybe you're worried that you're going to panic at the movie theater on your date night with your husband, and he reassures you that you'll sit on the aisle where it's easy to leave if you begin to panic. That calms you down for a minute, but then you suddenly think, "Wait! What if we get to the theater late and all those seats are taken?" Or maybe you're anxious about making friends when you start college in the fall. Your older sister tells you, "Don't worry! College is nothing like high school—everyone's really nice." Hearing this, you feel relieved—until it occurs to you that your sister has always been more outgoing than you, and maybe making college friends is even harder than making high school friends when you're shy.

The *right* reassurance is reassurance that you are competent to
handle problems. You don't feel better when people tell you "everything
will be fine!" without addressing the

> *The* right *reassurance*
> *is reassurance that*
> *you are competent to*
> *handle problems.*

content of your worry. But you will get some relief from your
worry if you remind yourself that even if the worst does happen, you'll be able to deal with it.

At this point, you need to include others in your effort to
contain worry. People you turn to for support and reassurance
need some information to help you make good progress. You
need to tell them what's helpful to hear—and what's not.

Reassurance for Generalized Anxiety

The first step here is to get the worry out in the open so you
can see if it's connected to a real problem or is simply the result
of your overactive, anxious brain.

Once the problem is defined, the right reassurance is reassurance that you're competent to handle the problem, should it
occur: "If it turns out there is a problem, you'll figure out what
to do." Here are a couple of examples of the right reassurance
and the wrong reassurance for generalized anxiety.

Wrong Reassurance	*Right Reassurance*
That could never happen. Here's why . . .	If this is a real problem, you'll figure out what to do.
Just stop worrying! This is nonsense!	You can manage your worry. Focus on that.

Reassurance for Panic

The right reassurance for panic is not "Oh, you won't panic." It is "If you should panic, even if it's a lot of panic, you have all the skills you need to cope with it." Of course, you do actually need those skills for this reassurance to work, so make sure you've practiced Anxiety Buster 2 (Breathe) and Anxiety Buster 5 (Don't Make Mountains Out of Molehills).

The first step for getting the right reassurance for panic is to acknowledge that your fear is (1) that the panic will be horrible, and (2) that the outcome will be awful. In fact, neither catastrophe is true. It may be true that if you panic, you'll feel embarrassed or want to escape—but that's a far cry from the dying, going crazy, or losing control that you fear.

Then, remind yourself that you are competent to handle your panic and its consequences. Here are some more examples of the right reassurance and the wrong reassurance for panic.

Wrong Reassurance	*Right Reassurance*
You won't panic!	If you panic, you know what to do to calm down.
You have nothing to be scared of!	Even if you panic, you'll get through it.
	If you panic, you can go on with what you were doing once it's over.

Reassurance for Social Anxiety

Because people with social anxiety are especially sensitive to feelings of anxiety, they're more inclined to fear feeling anxious. They particularly fear other people noticing they are nervous. If you have social anxiety symptoms, you'll need the social skills to accomplish your goals—and the practice to make them work well. Pay special attention to Anxiety Buster 10.

At the beginning, the right reassurance for people with social anxiety is, "You're working on your goals, and I can help you with that." Once you've worked on your anxiety-reduction plan and practiced it, the right reassurance might be: "Even if you show some anxiety, you know how to get through it. And remember, people are more accepting than you may think."

In general, the right reassurance for social anxiety includes

(1) openly acknowledging what exactly you think will happen, and (2) reminding yourself that you have the competence to handle both your fear and the consequences of feeling afraid (showing signs of nervousness). Here are some examples of the right reassurance and wrong reassurance for social anxiety:

Wrong Reassurance	*Right Reassurance*
No one can tell that you're nervous.	You can tolerate anxiety or nervous feelings.
There's nothing to worry about.	Even if you look a little nervous, you can handle it.

Make a Plan

People with anxiety are often extremely competent in handling real problems. Real problems have real solutions, and a clear plan of action is a godsend to an anxious mind.

Consider your typical type of worry: "What if my car breaks down on vacation?" "What if I fail the test?" "What if no one asks me to the prom?" "What if I don't get this job I applied for?" All of these situations have a common element—if they do happen, a response will be in order, and in each case, a plan could be made. But worriers sometimes get confused about the difference between things that might require action and unnecessary worries. If you can't identify a specific problem that can be solved, then you're probably just having an anxious thought, and Stop and Swap is in order. For example, ruminatively thinking, "What if I lose my job?" may be a pointless (though disturbing) worry if you have a secure job in a stable company. But if you're worrying about a real situation—"My company is going to lay off 30% of the workforce, and one of those people could be me"—then you have an actual potential problem that can be addressed by coming up with a plan.

Even when there is a real situation that can be addressed by a plan, however, some people simply worry about the situation without moving to the next step of identifying the actual problem. Mandy was a good example of that. She called me in distress, saying, "I lost my job!" and asked for an emergency appointment. When she came in, I asked her what she wanted to discuss. She was taken aback. "I lost my job!" she exclaimed, wondering if I heard her the first time. "Yes," I replied, "but how is that a problem?" With a look of puzzlement on her face, she said carefully, "I . . . lost . . . my . . . job." "Indeed. And how does losing your job cause a problem in your life?" Then it dawned on her: "Oh. Because I lost my job, now I have the problem of needing another source of income." As a reader, you may be thinking, WELL, THAT'S OBVIOUS! LOSING YOUR JOB

IS THE SAME AS NEEDING A NEW SOURCE OF INCOME. But don't be quick to leap to such conclusions. Instead, consider Althea, who also lost her job. Althea had worked at a nonprofit organization that supported the arts. Married to a doctor, she didn't need to work for financial reasons—she worked because it provided her with a sense of purpose in life and because the job gave her status in the community. Both Mandy and Althea had lost their jobs, but their problems were very different, as were the solutions. To solve her problem, Mandy needed to find a new source of income. Althea, on the other hand, needed to find a new way to give her life purpose, possibly by doing volunteer work or taking up a new activity.

> *Some people simply worry about the situation without moving to the next step of identifying the actual problem.*

By getting stuck on the situation—"I lost my job"—you can feel desperately worried but unable to resolve your anxiety because you haven't defined the problem. Once you've identified the problem, you can begin figuring out a plan to address it, which will be a big relief to your anxious mind. Here's how to do that.

Step 1: Identify the Problem

What is the problem? Get very specific—for example, "I want a shot at a scholarship and I have three Bs. I want to raise them to As." Or "I want to go to the winter dance with a date and I have not yet been asked."

Step 2: What's the Goal?

Now, what is the goal? Goals direct solutions. Suppose your problem is that you haven't been asked to the winter dance. There could be several different goals associated with this problem. One might be: "I want to go to the dance with Michael." A very different goal might be: "I don't want to sit at home feeling lonely while my friends are at the dance." Each of these goals would lead to a different solution. In the first case, you might not want to accept any invitation to the dance unless it's from Michael. In the second, you probably would accept any invitation to the dance—or just decide to go without a date.

Step 3: Brainstorm About Solutions

What are possible solutions to achieve your goal? Write down every option—even "bad" ones you'd never choose. Anxiety narrows your thinking because it puts blinders on your attention and creativity. Sometimes listing wrong choices makes it easier to see the right one.

Also, a lot of anxiety is generated by feeling that you have no choice or control in a situation. But you always have a choice, even if the choice is to continue on the path you're already on.

Another trick your mind might play on you is: "What if I didn't think of everything?" To circumvent this, ask yourself, "Is there anything else I have to consider or do?" If you answer, "No, this should cover it all," then your worry, "What if I didn't think of everything?" is just a trick your anxious brain is playing on you. Say to yourself, "I will not replan my plan. I will evaluate my progress on _____." Then do Stop and Swap.

Step 4: Select One Option

Now pick one "best" solution and identify the action steps you'll need to follow to do it. Remember: You are picking the best solution—not the perfect solution! People often get stuck worrying, "What if I choose wrong?" But the truth is this: There are many good solutions; there is no perfect solution. Say to yourself instead, "I can change my mind later if my evaluation shows this solution is ineffective." This is the purpose of evaluation!

> *There are many good solutions; there is no perfect solution.*

Step 5: Tell Yourself: "Stop! I Have a Plan!"

Expert worriers may find themselves worrying even after they have a plan. This is where Stop and Swap comes in. If you feel those "what if" thoughts popping back up, tell yourself "Stop!" and then add, "I have a plan!" Then use your planned-ahead thought replacement.

Step 6: Evaluate How the Plan Is Working

It is necessary to plan evaluation points. If you don't, you'll just continue to worry: "Is this the right step? Is this working? What if it doesn't work?" Remember, you are evaluating your progress—not whether the problem has been completely resolved. Depending on your goal, achieving the solution may take some time. But working toward that goal is something you can begin immediately, noting whether you've been successful in achieving each of the action steps on the path to solving the problem. Decide which action steps need evaluation and when.

Here's how to do it:

1. Decide what the first reasonable point to evaluate your progress is, and mark it down on your calendar. For example, if your goal is to find a new job, a reasonable first evaluation point might be in 2 weeks. ("Have I sent out my

resumé to at least five different companies? Have I received any requests for interviews?") If your goal is to mend a friendship with someone you had a falling out with, your first evaluation point might be quite a bit later. Don't monitor daily unless it's called for—that's just another way of letting "what if" thinking creep in. If you notice yourself doing this, say, "Stop! I will think about this on _____" and then do a thought replacement.

2. If obstacles come up, you can revise your action steps.

3. Evaluate the results on the day you marked in your calendar.

- If you were successful, note what you did to make it work.
- If you were unsuccessful, either revise your action steps or consider trying a different solution option.

4. After evaluating your results, set a new evaluation date and mark it on your calendar. Continue with this process until the problem is solved.

Finally, when evaluating your progress toward your goal, look at what's working! What is going right? How did you make that happen? What do you want to adjust to make it better? Stay far away from what is wrong or not perfect.

Worry Well and Only Once

People with anxiety disorders worry when worry is unnecessary, worry when there is no value in worrying, and, mostly,
worry to the extent that it ruins their lives. Worry Well and
Only Once is a method that takes worry seriously one time
only and sorts out real problems from unrealistic worries. It
involves examining what you can control versus what you can't.
And it helps you make arrangements for when it would be a
good idea to worry again.

Worry Well and Only Once works best for situations that
are serious and have a measure of ambiguity, such as when
you're undergoing medical treatment, experiencing legal trouble, or waiting to hear whether you passed the state bar exam.

Here's the process:

1. Start by listing all the things you could be worried about.
   Dissect your problem.
2. Then, do anything that must be done at this time and do
   not delay. Make phone calls, talk to someone, write or
   make something, repair, clean, or take any action that will
   improve the situation.
3. Sometimes taking action is necessary only if the problem
   should occur. In that case, make a plan "in case it occurs."

4. Ask yourself, "Is there anything else I need to worry about?" Your brain needs to hear a "no." If you say yes, redo steps 1–3.

5. Set a time when it will be necessary to think about the worry again, and write it down somewhere: "If x happens, then I will do y. But if x does not happen, the next time I will review this worry is on March 15." (Note this on your calendar: "Worry about x.")

6. Whenever the worry pops up again, declare, "Stop! I already worried!" and use a thought replacement.

Ditch Your Dread

The sensation of dread can precede the thought that there is something to feel dreadful about. Sometimes this is referred to as "free-floating" anxiety, but it can be recognized by the pit-of-the-stomach unease that all people associate with dread. The circle of dread is shown on the next page.

If you feel dread, this method is going to be of considerable use to you. But be forewarned: It requires a leap of faith—you must believe that dread can precede worry and be present for no good

> *For many with generalized anxiety, it is dread that creates the worry—not the other way around.*

reason. Although worry can indeed make you full of dread, for many with generalized anxiety, it is dread that creates the worry—not the other way around. The sensation of doom is an outcome of your brain's biology. But it's simple to get rid of.

1. The first step is to come to believe that you will not fail to notice a real problem.
2. Next, notice the dread. Don't try to figure out why you're feeling the dread. Instead, simply ask, "Is this sensation dread?"

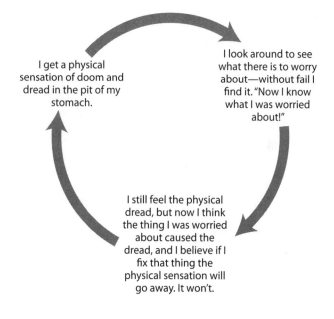

I get a physical sensation of doom and dread in the pit of my stomach.

I look around to see what there is to worry about—without fail I find it. "Now I know what I was worried about!"

I still feel the physical dread, but now I think the thing I was worried about caused the dread, and I believe if I fix that thing the physical sensation will go away. It won't.

3. Then, find a way to relieve the sensation:
   - Through diaphragmatic breathing (Anxiety Buster 2). With just a minute to breathe and engage in muscle relaxation, the body can relax and begin to let go of the dread at the physical level.
   - Through Stop and Swap (Anxiety Buster 6). Say to yourself, "Stop! I won't fail to notice a real problem." Then immediately use a thought replacement.

The following statements will help you ditch your dread. On an index card, write down the one that most appeals to you and then carry the card with you.

- A feeling is just a feeling.
- Dread does not need a reason. I will not go on scan mode to find one.
- Breathe, distract.
- I won't fail to notice a real problem. I don't have to look for one.

Clear Your Mind

Do you feel your mind jumping around or find it hard to stop it from running down a track? Do you need to:

- Get everything off your mind to focus on something important, like studying for a test or writing a report for work
- Clear away tangled thoughts to think clearly about something
- Empty your mind to rest
- Leave work behind to enjoy time off or come into the house ready to be home

If this is what you need, Clear Your Mind is the method for you. There are several versions, but all are simple.

The Container

The Container method goes like this:

1. Imagine a container sitting in front of you. It's a container that can hold all your concerns. The container is open and ready to receive whatever you want to put into it.
2. Now, think about (but don't mull over) all the things that are pressing on your awareness or asking for your attention. Anything—good or bad, big or small—can go into the container. Give each thing a name.
3. When everything has been named and put in the container, place the lid on the container and set it aside.

4. If the next thing you want to do is sleep, invite a peaceful thought into your mind.
5. If you want to focus on something, invite into your mind thoughts about what your focus is.

Other Versions

Some people are not fond of the container imagery, and if that's the case for you, or if you just want more than one way to clear your mind, here are other ways to use this method:

- *The list.* Write down your thoughts in the form of a list. Be very brief, using only one or two words for each. Then put the list in a drawer, briefcase, or other place where it will literally be out of sight (and out of mind).
- *The God Box.* This version comes from Al-Anon. The God Box is used to hold slips of paper, each of which have a thought that is to be turned over to God.
- *Pictures in a backpack.* This version works best with children. They can write or draw a picture of their thoughts or worries and put it into a worry backpack, worry box, or worry file that a counselor or teacher keeps for them. With that adult, they can periodically open the backpack and see what's in it. They will learn that worry passes, and if bad things happened, they lived through them and coped.

- *Worry dolls.* These are small Guatemalan dolls in a box or bag that can be purchased from global marketers or import stores. The legend is that a person can hand the concerns or worries of life over to the dolls and the dolls will take the worries away. The lid is literally put on the box so that the dolls can carry the worry away and ready themselves for the next batch of worries.

"ARE THERE SPECIFIC doctors there that you're concerned about?" Adam's friend Nancy asked as she bent down to retie the shoelace on her sneaker.

"Well, no," Adam said, "but I haven't met all of them, obviously."

"Then it's not a problem—at least right now." A pair of joggers passed them on the path, smiling hello as they passed. "If she goes into labor while her doctor's on vacation, and if whoever's there instead of him seems incompetent, you'll be able to tell. You've always been good in emergencies—remember when Beth cut her hand on the boat? You'll know if you need to get someone else in, or call her doctor, or whatever. You're great at that type of thing." Talking to Nancy always calmed Adam down. "I have a book you might really like," Nancy added. "I'll give it to you when we get back to my house."

That night, Adam sat down with the book and a cup of tea. "Worry well." He was already good at that, he thought wryly. "And only once." That last part might take more work.

Adam started by listing everything that worried him: A substitute doctor would make a mistake. Something would go wrong with the delivery. Something would be wrong with the baby.

There was nothing he really could do about any of these possible problems right now, so he made a plan for what he would do if they did happen: Find out, ahead of time, if the hospital would be able to reach the primary obstetrician on his cell phone during the birth, and if something seemed to be going wrong, insist that they call him immediately. Research the other doctors at the hospital to find out which were best, and have their names ready so he could request them for a second opinion.

And if something was wrong with the baby? Well, that one would harder to solve, especially without knowing ahead of time what was wrong. But he could make a point of supporting Rachel and Eli emotionally, and he could help out financially as well.

Was there anything else he needed to worry about? Adam took a sip of tea and looked out the window. Well, there was the remote possibility that things would go horribly wrong, and the baby—or Rachel—would die. He didn't want to think about it, but if it happened, he could help make arrangements for the funeral service and the burial. He could pick up some of Rachel and Eli's household responsibilities—cooking, cleaning, paying bills—for as long as he was needed. He could ask Nancy to help him find a group therapy program for grieving.

Adam sat down at his dining room table and began writing a list of his worries: BAD SUBSTITUTE DOCTOR. PROBLEMS WITH DELIVERY. BIRTH DEFECTS. RACHEL DIES. BABY DIES. With a pair of scissors, he carefully cut the items apart from each other and then placed them in a jewelry box he'd given Beth on one of their wedding anniversaries. He closed the lid and put the box back on the shelf. "Tell me what to do, Beth," he whispered under his breath, "if I need it." Then he went to bed, with a plan to worry again at the same time the next week, and quickly slipped into a deep sleep.

He awoke when his cell phone rang at three in the morning. It was Eli. Adam picked up the phone.

"It's showtime!" Eli sounded giddy. "See you at the hospital."

Fourteen hours later, Adam was holding his grandchild—a perfect 7-pound, 3-ounce baby girl, screaming at the top of her little lungs.

Think Something Different, Do Something Different

H<small>E COULD'VE KILLED</small> her! His sister Lizzy had put up a profile for him on a popular Internet dating site, and now Shane was getting at least 10 messages a week from interested women. "You're 29 years old," Lizzy had scolded him when he called to complain about what she'd done. "And you've never had a real girlfriend. It's insane! I know meeting people makes you nervous, but it's time to man up!"

Shane clicked onto the page that Lizzy had written for him and read it again. The pictures she'd posted could have been worse, but "I'm looking for someone who's outgoing but also enjoys a quiet night at home"? "My sense of humor is almost as good as my jump shot"? He never would brag like that! And his jump shot wasn't all that great.

The whole thing was mortifying. He wasn't looking for anyone. He'd had a couple of brief, casual relationships with girls back in college, but aside from that he'd had only one real date, and he didn't care to repeat the experience. Halfway through dinner, she'd laughed when he couldn't remember the name of his favorite band, and he was so embarrassed that he left before he'd even finished the meal.

"She wasn't laughing *at* you," Lizzy had said. "She was laughing because forgetting the name of your favorite band is, well . . . funny." Yeah, right.

Another notification of an incoming message popped up. Shane started to delete it but paused when he saw the woman's picture. She was cute. And her picture wasn't a selfie of her wearing next to nothing, or of her posing coyly with a flower tucked behind her ear. "I haven't actually ever written anyone through one of these sites," her message said, "but there was something about your profile that I liked. Coffee? Hope to hear from you. Ingrid."

Coffee. Hmm. Getting a coffee might be okay—he

could leave quickly if he felt too uncomfortable. Shane looked at her picture again. He pressed the reply button.

"Dear Ingrid," he typed. "Thank you for your message." He paused again. "Dear Ingrid, thank you"? It sounded like he was applying for a job. He deleted what he'd written. "Hi Ingrid. My sister actually put my profile up—I can't take any credit for it! But coffee sounds good." Figuring she'd never write back, Shane quickly pressed send.

His stomach clenched when Ingrid replied immediately. "The Leaf and Bean on 9th Street? Sunday afternoon?"

"Sure," he forced himself to write back. "What time is good for you?"

There's no question about it—experiencing social anxiety or a panic attack is terrifying. But fear *of* that fear is what's truly destructive, because it causes you to begin changing your life.

If going on a date has made you sick to your stomach, you probably now avoid meeting anyone new. If you've found yourself stammering at company meetings, you probably

> *Experiencing social anxiety or a panic attack is terrifying. But fear of that fear is what's truly destructive, because it causes you to begin changing your life.*

avoid talking at those meetings. If you've had a panic attack on an airplane, bus, or train, you probably avoid public transit. Avoidance may help keep your anxiety at bay, but it also keeps you from meeting new people, climbing the ranks at work, or getting where you need to go. And it keeps you from developing skills to deal with discomfort and to try doing things in a different way.

Much of the impact of fear lies in the way you think about it. And the way you think about fear has to do with what's called "self-talk"—the running dialogue you have with yourself in your head. By teaching yourself to think differently—to change that negative self-talk—you help yourself to behave differently. And once you begin thinking and behaving differently, you can get your life back on track.

Assess Your Avoidance

Avoidance of certain places and situations may begin at a fairly low level. Not going to the movies because you once had a panic attack at a theater, for example, may not be a terribly big sacrifice in the broad scheme of things. But avoidance behaviors tend to escalate, and soon you're avoiding not only cinema complexes but also concert halls and restaurants and even the auditorium where your daughter is receiving her high school diploma.

Are Avoidance Behaviors Beginning to Impinge on Your Life?

Check the questions that you can answer yes to:

❑ Do you stay away from places where you might have a panic attack?

❑ When you go into a new setting, do you check how you can escape?

❑ Do you avoid television shows or news reports about topics that raise your anxiety?

❑ Do you avoid thinking about topics that make you feel anxious?

❑ Do you make an effort to avoid being observed or being the center of attention?

❑ Do you worry ahead of time about what a new situation will be like and sometimes go to check it out ahead of time to reduce your anxiety?

If you checked yes for even one of these questions, you need to specifically identify your arenas of avoiding. Make a list of situations, places, or interactions with others that you have avoided. Here are some examples of common things people avoid:

- Going into large lecture classes at college
- Traveling by air

- Driving on a limited-access highway
- Going to the grocery store during the day
- Speaking in class or at a meeting
- Meeting new people (at work, at a meeting, at a party)

Identify Your Goals

Changing behavior starts with the conviction that behavior change is necessary. Is your avoidance behavior getting in the way of your goals? What do you want? To be able to go to a job interview? To be able to participate in class? To speak up at a meeting or point out your successes as your peers do?

Knowing what you have to gain by facing fear or anxiety is the first step to sticking with a plan for change. Because avoiding what you fear works very well to diminish anxiety, people who get a lot of relief when they avoid nerve-wracking situations must be clear about how they will benefit if they face the fear and do what scares them. And writing it down reinforces that knowledge. So take

Knowing what you have to gain by facing fear or anxiety is the first step to sticking with a plan for change.

a moment here to write down your goals. What will you be able to do if you have less anxiety? What quality of life are you seeking?

When you can see what your goals are, it's time to look at what is stopping you. How is your self-talk interfering with getting rid of anxiety? You may be telling yourself that your anxiety is impossible to control, or that panicking means you're going crazy. Let's take a look at your self-talk.

Assess Your Self-Talk

Again, self-talk is the running dialogue you have with yourself in your head. It's when you argue both sides of a problem with yourself, and it includes hearing in your mind the voice of a parent, coach, or acquaintance.

All too often our self-talk expresses criticism and doubt. "Should I try to talk to that attractive woman at the end of the bar? I guess not—I'm sure she wouldn't be interested in me, and I'd probably say something dumb." "Should I accept my friend's invitation to go to the baseball game? The last time I was in a stadium, I panicked, and I'll probably panic again. I guess I should tell him I can't go."

Is Your Self-Talk a Problem?

Check the questions that you can answer yes to:

❑ I tell myself that I will make a fool of myself if I try something new.

❑ I tell myself that people will not like me.

❑ I tell myself that no one else answers questions incorrectly or stumbles when trying to explain things in meetings or classrooms.

❑ I tell myself that I won't be able to stand it if others notice me blushing or getting embarrassed.

❑ I tell myself people won't notice if I don't show up or participate, so it's okay if I don't go to the event.

❑ I tell myself that I will feel scared and that I can't stand feeling scared.

If you checked yes to two or more of these questions, you need to learn how to begin changing your negative self-talk.

Negative self-talk increases fear and anxiety and makes us anticipate failure and rejection. The biggest problem with self-talk, especially when we don't realize we're doing it, is that it has the ring of truth. You tend to believe what you say to yourself.

And self-talk is predictive. If you tell yourself that something is going to be scary, chances are excellent that you will perceive it as scary. Your brain will then go on to warn you that every similar situation will be scary. And a self-fulfilling prophecy about social fear or panic is born.

However, if you deliberately make positive self-statements, you may well start to believe them instead! That's the goal of this technique.

Think Something Different: Find and Change Your Negative Self-Talk

It's important to remember that anxiety is a protective response. Your brain and body try to protect you by warning you of possible risks.

For example, if you're hiking in the woods and suddenly come face-to-face with a hungry bear, you're probably going to feel very anxious. Your heart rate will jump, and your brain will tell you, "Run! You're not capable of fighting off this bear!" That response works to keep you safe much of the time.

The problem is when your brain and body send out "Danger! Warning!"

The problem is when your brain and body send out "Danger! Warning!" signs when the situation isn't actually risky.

signs when the situation isn't actually risky. Your brain might warn you, for instance, to stay away from a dinner party you've been invited to because you might embarrass yourself. Or that you're not competent to handle the anxiety you might feel on an airplane. You have to learn to talk back to that warning.

Changing self-talk will help you:

- Learn to tolerate uncomfortable sensations as merely uncomfortable, not awful
- Take control of negative self-talk and eliminate it
- Act in direct opposition to false beliefs you hold about your competence
- Develop confidence that you can control fear and stop avoiding life

To change your negative self-talk, every small thought that creates anxiety must be identified and corrected. So how can you find out what you're saying to yourself?

Ask Yourself, "Why Am I Having These Symptoms?"

Do you talk to yourself in self-sabotaging ways? To hear your own voice, start out by being a detective in your own life. As you go through experiences, try to objectively notice exactly what happens and what you are saying to yourself. Write down everything so you don't overlook any important details. Copy down the following questions on an index card (or put them in your smartphone) and carry it with you at all times:

1. Notice: Where am I and what am I doing?
2. Notice: What are my anxiety symptoms and how bad are they?
3. Ask yourself: "Why am I having these symptoms?"

Your answer to this last question will reveal your negative self-talk. For example, one of my clients, Joseph, suffered from social anxiety. He sought therapy with me after discovering that he was in danger of failing an important college seminar course because he wasn't contributing to class discussions. Joseph's answer to the first question was, "I am in the seminar course. I'm listening to all the other students talk but I'm staying silent." In response to the second question, Joseph said, "I feel tense all over my body. When I think of something to contribute to the discussion, my heart starts to pound and I feel dizzy." His answer to "Why am I having these symptoms?" was, "My heart is pounding because whatever I have to say is probably dumb. And even if it's not dumb,

I probably won't be able to express it well enough for everyone else to understand."

Counter Negative Self-Talk

Once you know what you're telling yourself, you have to replace it. One way of doing this is to counter negative statements with their opposites.

Start by dividing a piece of paper into three columns. At the top of the first column, write "Goals." This is where you'll identify each part of an activity or situation that you want to do.

At the top of the second column, write "First Thought (Negative Self-Talk)." This is where you'll write down the negative thoughts you have about that specific goal.

Finally, at the top of the third column, write "Positive Replacement Thought." The thoughts you write in this column are the ones you'll read or say aloud the moment you have the negative thought.

Take a look at how this worked for Guy, a 22-year-old who wanted to go back to college after he had dropped out due to anxiety. He knew he had the intelligence to go to school, and it bothered him that he was working in a gas station when he could be in school.

Goals	First Thought (Negative Self-Talk)	Positive Replacement Thought
Start school in 6 weeks.	I may not be able to meet that timeline. I always miss deadlines.	I have filled out applications before and I know I have time to do this. I will use my support system to encourage me.
Talk to admissions about getting credits accepted.	I don't know where to go and I don't know whom to talk to there. It might not even be worth it—I bet they won't transfer credits from the junior college.	I can call ahead to get the information about whom to see and where to go. Other students figure it out, so I can too. I can't know what they will accept if I don't ask. It's worth it financially to make this effort, even if I don't like it.
Talk to other students.	I will make a fool of myself. I'm bad at talking to strangers.	All the students will be strangers to one another. Talking about class does not require me to be witty or tell jokes—just to talk, which I can do.

Goals	First Thought (Negative Self-Talk)	Positive Replacement Thought
Attend every class and not leave because I am nervous.	I've always left class when I'm anxious.	Even if I'm nervous, I can stay. I've practiced skills to stay.
Finish school completely in 2½ years.	I will never finish school. I don't think I will ever stay long enough to get enough credits.	Things are different today. I have a goal, and I can stay in school even if it's hard.

Recite Affirmations

People often fail for the simple reason that they believe they'll fail. If you have anxiety, you fail in advance by avoiding anything that seems too tough.

Your chances of success are much better if you imagine yourself succeeding. By affirming what you want to be true (about your life, your situation, your character, your attitudes) you create the conditions for that truth.

Affirmations counteract negative self-talk. An affirmation is a

> *Your chances of success are much better if you imagine yourself succeeding. By affirming what you want to be true, you create the conditions for that truth.*

151

positive statement about yourself, said aloud it as if it's already true. For example, if you want to become more comfortable talking at meetings, your affirmation might be, "I'm confident and competent when I express myself at staff meetings." You say the affirmation as if it's true right now.

Of course, for affirmations to be helpful, they must be believable and possible. Telling yourself, "I'm fully capable of jumping off the high dive" when you don't even know how to swim won't do you any good! First you need to learn to swim— or gain skills in public speaking if that's your fear, or learn the new computer software at work if you're anxious about your job performance. Once you have the skill set you need, proceed with the affirmation.

Take Off Your Dark Glasses

If you have panic or social anxiety, you probably tend to remember only the times you fled a room feeling like you were going to suffocate, or only the times you became embarrassed. You obsess about wrong answers you gave at school, the bad throws in the game, or the times you froze and didn't speak when you should have. If you have generalized anxiety, you may remember only the times when your dread did precede something bad happening.

But the fact is, you've probably succeeded far more often than you've failed, and 99 times out of 100, your dread was just a false alarm and nothing terrible came to pass. Think about it. Have you really panicked *every* time you've been in a crowded room? No! Have you really said something embarrassing *every* time you've had a conversation with someone? Of course not! What happened the last time you had that sinking feeling of impending doom? Did you really end up getting fired? Or get into a car accident? Or receive news that a family member had died unexpectedly? No, no, and no.

The problem with anxiety is that it puts you on the lookout for bad experiences, which means you overlook positive ones. You start going through life with dark glasses on, failing to notice the bright spots, the successes. Even worse, you start making inaccurate generalizations: "I panicked the last time I drove on the highway, so I will obviously panic whenever I drive on the highway." "I always say something stupid when I'm talking to people." Or you forget all the times your dread turned out

> *The problem with anxiety is that it puts you on the lookout for bad experiences, which means you overlook positive ones.*

to be a false alarm. When they go unchallenged, these mental errors—"I'll always panic"; "I'll say something stupid"; "My dread means something bad will happen"—seem to prove the self-talk true.

Do you have mental errors that need to be challenged? Do you tend to:

- Say, "I'm the only one who . . . "
  - "I'm the only one who ever trips in the hallway at school."
  - "I'm the only one who doesn't know which fork to use at a restaurant."
- Assume that what you fear will happen actually will happen.
  - "I know I'll panic if I go to the grocery store and it's crowded."
  - "I know I'll mess up if I raise my hand in class and try to answer."
- Have catastrophic expectations: "This will be the worst!"
  - "If I panic while I'm driving I could have a terrible accident."
  - "If I blush on a first date, she won't want to see me again."

Do you:

- Believe you can't tolerate negative experiences. ("If my boyfriend breaks up with me, I'll never get over it.")
- Believe you can't control how you feel.
- Believe you have no control over the outcome of situations.
- Believe you will inevitably feel rejected or embarrassed if others notice you.

To take off the dark glasses of anxious thinking, search for situations that disprove your negative beliefs. Whenever you feel anxious about an upcoming situation, make a mental note of it. Then, after the situation is over, write down what actually ended up happening.

- Were you able to be in a crowded room without panicking?
- Did people at the party not reject or humiliate you? (Important: Even though you might have felt embarrassed, did others *actually* reject or humiliate you? Saying that they were probably *thinking* negative thoughts doesn't count—you have no idea what they were actually thinking!)
- Did nothing bad end up happening despite your feeling a sense of dread?

Actually writing down these positive outcomes will help you remember them. And the more you remember them, the easier it will be to behave differently when your anxious thoughts crop up again.

Do Something Different: Tolerate Your Anxious Feelings

Using positive self-talk will help you stop your avoidance behavior. But it's not like flicking a switch and—voilà!—never experiencing anxiety again. To reengage in life, you need to learn to tolerate your anxious feelings.

What happens when you feel that first sensation of anxiety? That first tremor of your hand, or that first bit of queasiness in your stomach? You probably go from zero to sixty: "Oh no! There it is again! I know I'm going to panic!" or "Oh, no . . . something must be really wrong." Then you do what you've done before to escape, avoid, or otherwise react to your anxious feeling.

This method is about slowing down that rapid-fire response. It will help you become aware of your physical feelings without dramatizing or being afraid of them.

1. Sit comfortably in a chair with your feet on the floor.

2. Close your eyes and let your breath become even and regular.

3. If you're aware of any sensation in your body, just notice it—don't judge it as good or bad or try to analyze it.

4. If you don't immediately notice a sensation, slowly move your attention through your body—head . . . throat . . . shoulders . . . arms . . . fingers . . . chest . . . solar plexus . . . abdomen . . . back . . . legs . . . feet—and pause when you find a feeling in each.

5. Give each sensation you feel a physical description. Don't give it an emotional word like "scared" or "troubled," and don't decide if it's a good or bad sensation. Simply give it a physical label, such as tingling, shaking, fluttering, stabbing, tightening, or any other physical word that fits.

6. You'll know you've gotten the right label when your body gives you a response such as, "Ah, yes—that's it." If you don't get that kind of response after a moment, go back and forth with some similar words to see if one of them fits a little better.

7. Once you've gotten the right label, let your attention move away from the sensation. At this point you can think about

what it implies, you can note it for future thought, you can use the information to make a decision, or you can just return to the task at hand.

By labeling the sensations you feel in your body, you can begin to get familiar with them. And remember: Physical sensations don't demand action—they just give information. You don't need to do anything about them—you just need to be aware of them. As you get more comfortable noticing sensations without judging them, being afraid of them, or wanting to avoid them, you'll become increasingly confident that you can go into unfamiliar situations and change your behavior successfully.

> *Physical sensations don't demand action. You don't need to do anything about them—you just need to be aware of them.*

You'll also find that the better you get at tolerating your anxious feelings, the more they'll begin to subside. Why? Because you're teaching your brain to know the difference between a hungry bear in the woods and situations that aren't actually risky.

"SHE WOULDN'T HAVE written you if she didn't like your profile," Lizzy said when Shane called to tell her how anxious he was about his Sunday date. "I mean," she teased, "if she didn't like *my* profile of you."

Shane was unconvinced. "I'm going to write her back to cancel. I just don't see how I'll be able to have a normal conversation when all I'm thinking about is how not to throw up."

"Why would you feel like throwing up?" Lizzy asked. "You already know she's interested in you."

"Because I always end up saying something stupid, Liz! And it won't take long for her to realize that I'm just not that interesting."

"That's not true!" Lizzy argued. "How many guys do you know who went hiking by themselves through Central America? How many guys graduated college in three years while working part-time too?"

Shane was silent.

"Exactly. Look," Lizzy continued, "you just need to go into the whole thing with a different attitude. Focus on what you *can* do instead of what you can't. You can debate the pros and cons of decentralized markets. You can name every bird and animal native to Costa Rica."

"I don't know *all* the birds."

"See? You're doing it again!" Lizzy sounded exasperated. "You know *most* of them."

Shane sighed. "What if I throw up?"

"Seriously, Shane. When was the last time you actually threw up? And I don't mean when you had the flu."

"Yeah, but I feel like I'm going to."

"So what? Feeling like you're going to doesn't mean you actually will. Just tell yourself that you can get through it even if you're feeling anxious. Call me Sunday night to tell me how it went."

That Sunday, Lizzy picked up the phone on the first ring. "So? How did it go?"

"She said she wanted to see me again," Shane reported.

"And that was before or after you threw up on her?"

Shane chuckled. "It wasn't as bad as I thought it would be. Turns out she spent a semester in college volunteering at a sustainable farm in Costa Rica."

"See? I knew it! I knew you'd have something to talk about." Lizzy was triumphant. "You can make the check out for $50—I'm giving you a break on my matchmaking fee."

Shane smiled. "Sure, Sis. It's in the mail."

ANXIETY BUSTER

Control TMA (Too Much Activity)

A S SHE DROVE down the highway, Clara ran through the list of everything she needed to do that day. Pick up Bob's prescription at the pharmacy. Order a new karate uniform for Cole—6-year-olds grow so fast!—and call the school about setting the date for the fund-raiser. Stop by the church to meet with the new volunteers. Drop off the dry cleaning—and if there was time, squeeze in a manicure at the salon next door. Groceries for the barbecue tonight; get wine and beer at the liquor store—oh, and a few bottles of O'Doul's for . . . for . . . what was the name of the new associate at Bob's firm? Clara made a mental note to ask her husband about it when he got home.

Clara's cell phone rang. She fumbled one-handed

through her purse on the seat next to her, trying not to take her eyes off the road. Where was the dumb phone?! It stopped ringing just as she found it. A missed call from the assisted-living home they'd moved her father into a few months ago. Clara's stomach sank. She took the next exit off the highway, pulled over, and hit the callback button.

"Ms. Thorpe speaking," the voice chirped on the other end of the line.

"Hi, this is Clara MacDougal. Did you just call?"

"Oh, hello, Clara," Ms. Thorpe replied. "I just left you a message. I wanted to let you know—" she paused. "Well, don't worry, everything's fine now, but I wanted to let you know that we found your father wandering around the courtyard this morning. He was very disoriented. He's back in his room now, but we need to talk. We need to consider moving him to a facility that can provide more direct care."

Clara blew out a long sigh and rubbed the back of her neck. Whatever relief she felt that her father was safe was eclipsed by worry about his long-term health. "Okay. I was planning on coming in tomorrow. Can we talk then?"

"Sure, that's fine," Ms. Thorpe reassured her. "Would three o'clock work?"

Clara said yes and hung up. Springtime had arrived

in full force, with balmy days and everything in bloom, but all Clara felt was the knot in her stomach that just never seemed to loosen. Everything felt oddly heavy. Yes, coping with her father's declining health was stressful, and trying to get his finances in order was complicated, but otherwise her life was perfect: Bob had made partner. Cole had gotten into their first-choice private school. The town-beautification project she'd started through the church had become wildly successful. So why couldn't she shake this lingering sense of dread? She rubbed her eyes—carefully to avoid smudging her makeup—and pulled back into the road. WHAM! The car spun around, jerking Clara's head sideways, before it came to a halt on the sidewalk. Clara looked around, confused. A man was getting out of the other vehicle, cursing her as he approached her window.

Do people often say to you, "Where do you get the energy to do all that?" or "Don't you ever sleep?" If you get comments like these a lot, you may have what I call TMA—too much activity. People with TMA are always in overdrive, doing a million things at once. They get anxious when they're not actively working on something, but here's the rub: They also get anxious because they create too much to do.

You may be wondering, "What in the world could be wrong with being a high-drive, productive person?" Well, nothing, actually! You don't want to give up your level of productivity. You just want to give up the worrying that permeates your life. And here's the good news. You've already got so much energy that there's plenty to spare for making the Anxiety Busters work!

Assess Your TMA

You may not even recognize that you suffer from TMA, but the people around you certainly do! See where you fall on the TMA spectrum.

Do You Suffer From TMA?

For each of the following items, rate yourself on a scale of 1 to 5—with 1 being "not like me" and 5 being "very like me"—and then add the numbers for your total score.

1 2 3 4 5   Getting unexpected free time can raise my anxiety, especially if I have no warning.

1 2 3 4 5   I feel as if something is wrong if I'm not being productive.

1 2 3 4 5   My spouse or partner complains that I never sit down.

1 2 3 4 5   I'm secretly proud of how much I get done.

1 2 3 4 5   Efficiency is very important to me.

1 2 3 4 5   I become very impatient when something slows down my progress.

1 2 3 4 5   I get irritated when other people do something for me that I could have done myself and would have done better.

1 2 3 4 5   I feel stuck or frozen when my plans are disrupted.

1 2 3 4 5   I have trouble letting other people take over part of my work, whether it's at my job or in preparation for a social event (e.g., letting someone else grill the hamburgers).

1 2 3 4 5   I often spend energy on things that are important to me but neglect doing what's important to people who matter to me.

Total score _____

10–20 points = You don't have to worry about TMA.
21–30 points = Pay attention to your high drive. You're on your way to being out of balance and developing anxiety from TMA.

31–40 points = Your TMA is becoming excessive. You need to start taking control of your activities.

40–50 points = Your TMA is creating serious problems. Be on the lookout for stress-related health and emotional problems—you're on your way to burnout.

Are You a Student Who Suffers From TMA?

For each of the following items, rate yourself on a scale of 1 to 5—with 1 being "not like me" and 5 being "very like me"—and then add the numbers for your total score.

1 2 3 4 5   Getting unexpected free time can raise my anxiety, especially if I have no plan for what to do with the time.

1 2 3 4 5   I feel as if something is wrong if I'm not at an activity or doing homework.

1 2 3 4 5   I can only relax if I'm playing video games or doing something equally absorbing.

1 2 3 4 5   I don't talk about my good grades or successes with peers.

1 2 3 4 5   I get very upset if I forget assignments or get a bad grade.

1 2 3 4 5   Any bad grade makes me worry that I will fail the course (and a C would be a failure!).

1 2 3 4 5   I get irritated when I'm forced to work with a group of students because I end up doing it all or suffer because of their bad work.

1 2 3 4 5   I feel stuck or frozen when my plans are disrupted.

1 2 3 4 5   I feel the need to explain at length any poor performance in a nonclassroom activity, especially if other people notice it.

1 2 3 4 5   I repeatedly check with teachers, coaches, or faculty advisors to make sure I know their expectations.

Score _____

10–20 points = You don't have to worry about TMA.

21–30 points = Pay attention to your high drive. You're on your way to being out of balance and developing anxiety from TMA.

31–40 points = Your TMA is going to disrupt social relationships. Your anxiety is generated or made much worse by TMA.

40–50 points = Your TMA is creating serious problems and you may be feeling the impact on your self-esteem and social life. Be on the lookout for stress-related health and emotional problems—you're on your way to burnout.

Plan for Dreaded, Unexpected Free Time

Life always produces unexpected times when you have to hold still in one way or another. Appointments get canceled, people don't show up, airline flights are delayed, social events are postponed. If you have TMA, you probably find it challenging to hold still unexpectedly. It's as if you get brain freeze about what to do next. And you worry that you won't make the best choice about how to use that free time. The thought of not being 100% productive terrifies you.

If you have TMA, you probably find it challenging to hold still unexpectedly. It's as if you get brain freeze about what to do next.

The "if I ever have the time" list is a great way to relieve this anxiety. Whenever you say, "If I ever have the time, I want to _____," add that activity to the list, and keep the list handy. The activities you list can include anything at all—calling a friend, building shelves in the garage, putting together a scrapbook, taking a bath.

Try it now. Look around your home or office and see if you can find five things you will do if you ever have the time.

Now:

1. For each item, note how long it will take.
2. Carry the list with you, and whenever you're faced with dreaded unexpected free time, select an activity from the list that fits the available time.
3. As you complete tasks, cross them off and keep adding new "if I ever have time" items when you think of them.

Curb Perfectionism

People often use perfectionism to ward off anxiety, even if they don't realize it. The underlying belief is, "If I do enough, carefully enough, then I will never make mistakes and I won't have to worry." And this works well—until they do make a mistake. Then they have to raise the bar on being more careful and more thorough. And this, of course, reinforces the perfectionism.

People often use perfectionism to ward off anxiety, even if they don't realize it. The underlying belief is: "If I do enough, carefully enough, then I will never make mistakes and I won't have to worry."

You may fear that if you ever let down your perfectionist guard, things will completely fall apart and be absolutely, terribly wrong, and others will blame you entirely. (Note the extreme language here—it's the way the thought process goes.) In other words, you believe that everyone sees your mistakes as intolerable and as proof of your unworthiness.

So how do you curb this perfectionism? There are three steps.

Identify Your Perfectionism

To get a better sense of how perfectionism plays a role in your personal life, answer the following questions.

1. I have a strong sense of personal responsibility for the outcome of work-related, social, or family activities, even when other people could be reasonably expected to do some of the work. How do I show that?

2. I use extreme words like "always," "never," and "this is terrible," and I see the consequences of mistakes as being extreme (failure, ruin, etc.). Here are some examples: _____.

3. I'm very watchful about details. Here are the ways I am detailed oriented: _____.

4. I can't always see the difference between "good enough" and "perfect" when it comes to my responsibilities. Here's an example: _____.

See the Price of Your Perfectionism

Do any of the following apply to you?

- Have you been blamed (unfairly) for being controlling or have you been seen as not helpful?
- Have you taken on extra work that no one asked you to do and later felt overworked?
- Do you firmly believe you would have fun if you could only find the time?
- When you're responsible for an activity (such as hosting a party), do you feel a lack of pleasure and fun despite the fact that the activity should be fun?
- Do you feel completely exhausted and have no idea how or when you will recover?
- Are you noticing that you feel anxious, even when paying very close attention to details, in one arena of responsibility?

If you answered yes to even one of the above, it means your perfectionism is having negative consequences on your life. It's time to work less and figure out another way to let go of anxiety.

Change Your Pattern

Pick one of the following and commit to a specific way to try it in the coming week:

- Let others do a part of what you feel responsible for, even if you believe they won't do it as well.

- Every time you catch yourself using "all" or "never" language, tell yourself to stop it immediately. A mantra for anxious perfectionists should be: "Perfection is impossible." Follow that mantra with: "If something is impossible, then I have no obligation to try for it."

> *A mantra for anxious perfectionists should be: "Perfection is impossible."*

- Plan for nonperfectionism. Actually planning a nonperfect performance of some responsibilities will work better than noticing accidental imperfection. It won't be quite as anxiety provoking because you'll be doing it on purpose. Instructions for the perfectionist include:

- Let someone else step up to the plate (e.g., don't agree to mow the lawn just because your kid complains when you ask him to do it; don't agree to babysit at the last minute; don't write that report your colleague is dragging his feet on; don't agree to cover someone else's shift). You may find that when you hold back, someone else will step up. Even if the work doesn't get done, it's not the end of the world.

- Observe and evaluate how people respond to the imperfect work of others.
- Do not do work others are responsible for. Observe how this affects the attitudes of others and your own anxiety level.
- Finally, plan to not finish some work that you would otherwise have knocked yourself out to do. Miss a deadline by a little bit, or just don't do something. (Pick something that seems minor in the eyes of others. For example: Don't go out to buy the right napkins for the party—use paper towels. Or don't prepare the agenda in writing before the staff meeting.)

Now commit to doing it: I will _____ on this date or in this situation _____.

Finally, evaluate the outcome:

- Did anyone care whether I was perfect?
- If something went wrong unexpectedly, how did I and others cope?

- Can I tell the difference between the consequential things and inconsequential things? What did I note?

This evaluation will help you make future decisions about what you can drop and what is essential.

Get Back in Balance

"I know I should exercise and take care of my health, but. . . ." "I know I should spend more time with my kids, but. . . ." "I know it would be better if I took time for myself every day, but . . . ." Do these kinds of statements sound familiar to you? If so, you're lacking balance in your life, and it's time to get it back.

Of course, there are times when it's important to devote more attention to one part of your life. Maybe you're preparing to sell your company or getting your agency ready for inspection. Maybe you're studying for a final exam. Maybe you have a new baby. But shifting back to balanced activity after that period is over is often hard for people with TMA.

Is Your Life Out of Balance?
People with TMA can be very, very good at thinking they're sufficiently balanced, even when others in their lives don't see it that way. They need objective evidence. Here's a way to get it.

1. Keep track of what you're doing with your time for at least a week, every day. (If the week is not representative of your normal routine, do it for 2 weeks.)

2. Divide your week into hours, with 15-minute time slots in each day. Fill it in as you go—not at the end of the week—to keep from fooling yourself. Write down everything—brushing your teeth, watching television, eating, time with friends, writing work reports or e-mail, and even private things like sex. (You don't have to show the list to anyone!)

3. Now make a list of categories into which your daily activities fit (e.g., career, personal hygiene, hobbies, friends, family).

4. Add up the minutes you spent on the activities in each category.

5. Use these totals to create a pie chart showing the amount of time you spend on each category.

Does Your Use of Time Fit Your Values?

Now that you can see how you're spending your time, does the proportion make sense to you? Does it seem off balance? For example, are you spending more time on your career when you want to spend more with your kids? (Remember, though, that there are a limited number of hours in the day! We'd all love to spend lots of time with our kids and lots of time climbing the ladder at work, but that's not possible. Be realistic when you make this assessment.)

If you do decide that you're spending too little time on something you care about, begin to rebalance your life with this one method: Increase the time you spend on something you want very much to do, and spend less time on something that matters less.

Weigh the Importance

This method works well when you're evaluating just a couple of aspects of your life. It involves asking yourself two questions:

- How important is it that I do this task or activity?
- How important are all the things I am *not* doing in order to do this task or activity?

For example, suppose you're trying to decide whether to attend a conference out of town or stay at home with your daughter and husband. The conference is important for your work, so you rate it "very important." What are all the things you won't be able to do if you attend it? You'll miss your daughter's soccer game, you won't get to spend time with your husband, and you won't be able to plant that flower bed you've been meaning to get in. How important are those things? If you missed your daughter's last soccer game, and things have been strained with your husband, and you really miss the down time of gardening, maybe those things get ranked as "very, very important" and you decide to do them instead. On the other hand, if you've been to most of your daughter's games, and things are fine with your husband, and you'll have time to garden next weekend, maybe you rate the conference as more important.

Use Your Values to Make Decisions

If you're having a hard time making a decision in any situation in which you have to make a choice (whether to take a job, buy a house, go to one school versus another), it's probably because you're not taking your values into consideration. Try this:

1. Identify the situation (e.g., taking a new job).
2. List every important aspect of the situation that affects your decision (e.g., making money, prestige, relationships with colleagues, workplace environment, amount of responsibility).
3. Now sort the list according to a hierarchy of what is most significant. (Sometimes it's easy to see what's important, but sometimes it's not so clear. You can clarify your values by comparing one significant item to each of the others on your list: Is making money more important than pres-

tige? Is it more important than good relationships with colleagues?) Rewrite the list with the most important thing at the top.

4. Now make a decision. Ask, "Does this decision support the important things in my life?"

Have Some Fun

If you have TMA, you're probably overworked and underrelaxed. One client of mine, Betty, described it well. She said she liked to entertain. But she also said she didn't remember much about her parties because she was so busy being a nonstop perfect hostess. The fun was hearing that her guests enjoyed themselves. Classic TMA—too much work blotted out the fun.

Laughter Is a Good Start

Laughing is a great way to increase good feelings while discharging physical energy. Having fun and getting the relief of laughing is serious therapy for the serious person. Ask yourself, "What makes me laugh?"

> *Laughing is a great way to increase good feelings while discharging physical energy.*

Look for "Busy-Fun" Opportunities

Because people with TMA don't like to sit still, they often find busy-fun activities—like a 40-mile bike ride or hitting every garage sale in town on a Saturday morning—more relaxing than leisurely activities, such as a massage or soak in the tub. When choosing busy-fun activities, make sure you distinguish between those that are pleasurable to do and those that are pleasurable because they give you a sense of accomplishment afterward. The goal is to find activities that you enjoy as you actually do them.

"I'M FINE!" CLARA protested when Bob arrived at the hospital, demanding that they X-ray her sore shoulder. "I don't have time for all this! I still have to get groceries for the barbecue, and I have to stop by the church, and—"

Bob cut her off, with a look of astonishment on his face. "Clara, what are you *talking* about? You were just in a car accident! We're not having the barbecue tonight!"

Clara pushed her fingers against her eyes to keep from crying. "I just. . . ." Her voice trailed off. "I'm fine, really," she added softly.

Bob took her hand. "Look, I called your sister to pick up Cole from school. We can reschedule the barbecue, but we should have it catered instead. You need a break." Clara looked away and waved her hand dismissively. But she didn't argue when the X-ray clinician came in.

The next day, Clara awoke to the smell of bacon burning. Bob was already up, apparently attempting to make breakfast. She winced as she pulled back the covers to get out of bed. The X-rays may have come back clean, but she was definitely bruised.

"What time is it?" Clara asked as she entered the kitchen. "And where's Cole?" The pan of burned bacon was sitting on the cutting board. At least he'd taken it off the stove.

"I asked your sister to take him for the morning," Bob said. "We need to talk."

Clara sat down as Bob put breakfast—minus the bacon—on the table.

"I realize you've had to pick up a lot of slack with my work hours being what they've been." Bob looked at his wife. "And things with your dad have been stressful, to say the least. But when was the last time you did something just for yourself?"

Clara sighed.

"You don't even seem to enjoy the things you should be enjoying," Bob continued. "Like when you talk about the project with the church, it's just . . . well, like business, not fun."

"But it *is* like business, Bob. That project isn't going to organize itself." A hint of irritation tinged Clara's voice.

"I realize that, Clara, I really do. But you're planting trees and designing gardens, not digging ditches. It should feel like fun, too."

Clara sighed again. She had to admit that Bob was right.

"I think you need to take a hard look at what you're spending your time on," Bob continued. "And let some other people take up the slack once in a while. That accident could've been serious. How good are you going to be as a mom, daughter, project manager, and everything else if you're stuck in a hospital bed for months—or worse?"

That was definitely true. Of course, part of needing to do everything herself was because other people didn't do it as well as she did—the bacon being a case in point. But she'd gotten so wrapped up in getting everything done that she'd run herself ragged, and what good was she in that state?

Later that day, Clara made a decision. She'd figure out what was most important to her, spend most of her time on those things, and ask other people to help her with the rest.

Right off the bat, she knew that spending quality time with her father was the first priority. Why had she been putting in so many hours on getting his finances in order when just being with him was far more important? An accountant could be hired to straighten out the finances—she could check his work but let him do the bulk of it. Next was having some free time with Cole.

Maybe his karate lessons weren't that essential in the big scheme of things—if she canceled them, they'd have an extra few hours a week to spend at the playground just running around, having fun. And finally, the town-beautification project was her baby, but one of the volunteers was particularly good and had expressed an interest in getting more involved. Maybe Clara could ask her to take over some of the organizing so that she'd have more time to spend on the creative aspects of the project.

Clara felt an immediate sense of relief after reorganizing her priorities. But it was short-lived—letting the accountant take charge of her father's finances and letting the volunteer train the new volunteers caused a major spike in her anxiety. Still, Clara forced herself to tolerate those anxious feelings. "I'll give it a month and then see how things are going," Clara told herself. "I can always take over again if I need to." But after a month or so, she had to admit that they weren't doing a bad job. She still worried that taking Cole out of karate might hurt his chances of getting into future schools, but she'd spent some of their extra time together taking him to visit his grandfather, and in the end, those memories would be far more lasting than anything else.

ANXIETY BUSTER  **10**

Plan and Practice

THREE YEARS BEFORE she picked up the phone to make her first therapy appointment, Lark had everything she dreamed of: a coveted position as a buyer for a high-end housewares store, a husband she adored, a 7-year-old daughter who made her laugh every day, a nice house in a town that felt like home. But one April afternoon, her life took a sudden U-turn. She was in a department store trying on a pair of jeans when she heard what sounded like a car backfiring, followed by terrified screams. Instinctively, she dived under the dressing room chair and waited there for what felt like hours. When she finally came out, it was to phalanxes of reporters and the flash of cameras.

No one had actually been injured in the armed robbery, but everything felt different after that day. Life was no longer a given. Nothing was a given.

Lark's first panic attack came on without warning about 3 months later. She'd just gotten on an elevator when she suddenly felt short of breath. Not knowing what was happening made her panic even more—at the tenth floor, she bolted into the hallway, where she stood panting before slumping to the floor.

Soon it was apparent that any enclosed space—like the dressing room she was in when the robbery occurred—could trigger her panic: elevators, restrooms, even the little coffee shop on the corner where she liked to get scones. This was a problem at work, where the only route to her office was either up the elevator or the narrow stairwell to the fourth floor. Lark began dreading leaving home in the morning and started calling in sick—first only occasionally, but then more regularly. She convinced her manager to let her work from home half the week, but even with that, she still blew through all her sick days, and used some of her vacation days to stay at home as well. Now her job was on the line.

Family life was suffering, too. Things were okay when James and Celeste were home, but going out with them posed logistical challenges. What if she needed to use the restroom during the school play? She might panic in the stall. Going shopping with Celeste for clothes was totally out of the question—and that had been something she once really enjoyed with her daughter. Their annual summer camping trip was unthinkable, too. Now only James and Celeste went, because the mere thought of being inside the tent made Lark feel like she was going to pass out.

This week she was missing another chance to be with them. They'd flown down to Disney World, but Lark had stayed back because she didn't want to panic on the plane. Alone in the house, she finally decided to make the call to Dr. Baum. She missed James and Celeste terribly. And she missed her old life.

People develop panic disorder for all sorts of reasons. You may have experienced a trauma, like Lark did. Or your panic may have come out of the blue, seemingly prompted by nothing. Either way, you learned to be afraid by feeling afraid in a situation—whether it was actually risky or not. And your brain wants to make sure you stay out of scary situations in the future. So it sends the warning—"Caution! Danger! Don't go in there!"—whenever it gets nervous. And you obey it.

But most of the situations your brain begins to warn you about are harmless. There's no reason for you to keep avoiding them. That's why you need to teach your brain to unlearn that fear.

> *Most of the situations your brain begins to warn you about are harmless.*

If you want to unlearn fear—whether it's panic or social fear—you have to be in the frightening-but-harmless situation without feeling afraid. You have to be there without the scare! Just as you can legitimately learn fear by being caught in a genuinely dangerous situation, you can also legitimately unlearn fear by successfully exposing yourself to the harmless situation without succumbing to your fear.

Preparation is key here—you can't expect to quickly jump into real-life exposure. But with careful preparation, practice, and gradual exposure, you'll be able to unlearn your fear. That's what this Anxiety Buster is about. In order for it to work, though, you need to have practiced the other Anxiety Busters first. They will help give you the skill set you need to successfully carry out your plan.

Panic and Trauma

The techniques in this Anxiety Buster can be used by anyone, but if your panic is rooted in an earlier trauma, you need to also seek help from a therapist. A trained therapist can provide you with treatment and support that no book, no matter how good, can offer. Some of these trauma treatments include systematic desensitization, EMDR, energy therapies, and biofeedback or neurofeedback. These can be excellent choices to help with desensitizing, especially if you have a history of being shamed, bullied, humiliated, or terrified. It's not easy to bounce back from such life experiences without additional help.

Three Deep Breaths and Good Preparation

When I was in high school, I was stricken with vicious stage fright. Waiting in the wings to go onstage, I would pray to God to make me fall over dead before I had to go out and sing. Dying may not have been the best choice of avoidance behaviors, but it was the only excuse the rest of the cast would accept if I missed my cue!

My drama coach taught me one of the best anxiety-management ideas I would ever learn. Intuitively mastering diaphragmatic breathing because of her singing ability, she taught me to breathe slowly and deeply. She also gave me a mental framework for handling the anxiety, declaring, "All you need is three deep breaths and good preparation." Her "three deep breaths and good preparation" has become my model for getting rid of anxious behavior in any kind of anxiety-producing situation.

"Three deep breaths" stands for the ability to remain physically calm. It doesn't matter which breathing exercise you choose, or what kind of muscle relaxation you pair it with, as long as you use a physical calming technique when you face something that makes you anxious. (Review Anxiety Busters 2 and 4 to refresh your memory on physical calming techniques.)

"Good preparation" stands for all the stages of getting ready to practice in real life. Having worked on your self-talk in Anxiety Buster 8 will be very useful for this. Changing your self-talk lays the groundwork for successfully using the methods discussed here.

Step 1: Set Goals

Why in the world would someone who wants to die rather than sing a solo in front of an audience go out to sing more than once? Motivation! Once I got in front of the audience without dying, I enjoyed the act of singing. I had practiced it and I could do it well. And then there was the applause—it felt really good! With enough motivation, any person will face fear. And once you face your fear, it is diminished.

Knowing what you stand to gain increases your motivation to face your fear. It also helps you set goals.

> *Knowing what you stand to gain increases your motivation to face your fear.*

What are your goals? Are they something like these?

- To place an order in a restaurant without breaking into a sweat
- To speak to your boss without a quivering voice
- To stay in class this semester
- To start interviewing for jobs

Make a list of your goals. They can be very general or specific.

Step 2: Identify and Build the Skills You Need

No matter how specific or general your goals are, your next step is to see if you have the skills necessary to achieve them. If your social or work life is impeded by fear of panic, then controlling panic attacks is your first order of business (see Anxiety Busters 2 and 4). The other skills you'll need depend on the kind of anxiety you have. Here are a few examples.

Social Skills

- Meet new people, introduce yourself, and ask questions of others
- Eat in public or eat with unfamiliar people at the table
- Speak in community meetings such as the PTA
- Talk to teachers or administrative staff at your child's school
- Ask for a date or invite a new acquaintance to meet for coffee or lunch

Everyday Life Skills

- Competently drive or use public transportation
- Run errands or shop for groceries when stores are busy
- Be assertive enough to handle issues such as returning damaged goods or talking with customer service representatives
- Sign checks or credit card slips in front of a clerk
- Talk with retail personnel, asking questions about purchasing or exchanging goods
- Talk with medical personnel and clarify information about conditions and treatments

- Deal with insurance companies for claims and coverage concerns
- Talk with ease to your child's coaches or tutors or make appointments and financial arrangements for lessons

Work or Career Skills

- Ask questions of a supervisor about your work duties
- Ask for training on a job task that you cannot perform adequately
- Attend training sessions with or without colleagues present
- Independently obtain additional training by finding and attending certification or education programs available in the community
- Discuss schedule change requests with a manager
- Talk socially with a coworker at break
- Talk with a coworker about a work situation
- Enter a meeting room and choose where to sit; greet colleagues as they enter the room
- Make presentations at your job
- Offer comments during a group meeting
- Interview for a job

In identifying the skills you need, write down only the skills you don't actually have—don't include things you *can* do but don't enjoy doing. For example, you may be able to smile, shake a stranger's hand, and say, "It's nice to meet you" even if you don't particularly enjoy it. That means you do have the skills to meet new people.

Once you've identified the skills you need, finding outside help to build them is the next step. It's very important to be honest with yourself about what you need to learn—you'll never become truly confident unless you have the competence (skills) to back it up.

There are many ways to learn skills. Books are one way to go, but groups are also often available for learning specific skill sets, such as assertiveness, social skills, conflict management, or anger management. You may have to hunt to find a local therapist who offers these kinds of groups, but often it's well worth the effort. Look at adult education programs at community colleges for topics like public speaking, flirting, interviewing, etiquette, and Internet communication, as well as for one-time social opportunities (such as tours or theater performances) that give you a chance to be social with a focus for the conversation. These classes are often very inexpensive.

Step 3: Rehearse

Many people resist practicing, even in private, because they're embarrassed, but that's exactly why it's necessary! Not practicing before the real event is akin to memorizing a part in a play but never saying it aloud before going onstage. Not even a completely relaxed actor would want to go on without a rehearsal.

Identify Achievable Steps

You've already identified your goals. Some of them may be specific; others may be broader. For the ones that are broader, break the goal down into smaller, achievable steps.

For example, perhaps one of your goals is to learn to interview for jobs without looking nervous. This goal might be broken down like this:

1. Be able to greet the people interviewing me
2. Be able to talk about myself
3. Be able to ask and answer questions without looking nervous

Go ahead and break your goal down into smaller steps.

Now, break those steps down into even smaller steps. Smaller steps of "be able to greet the people interviewing me" might be (1) be able to shake hands and say hello, and (2) be able to maintain eye contact. Smaller steps of "be able to ask and answer questions" might be (1) make a list of questions and feel comfortable asking them, and (2) be able to pause and think, if a question requires it, without appearing nervous.

Identifying small steps that you can reasonably accomplish is the key to unlearning fear. Breaking off chunks too big for your temperament and skills is self-defeating. Make sure you can do each step before going on to the next one.

> *Identifying small steps that you can reasonably accomplish is the key to unlearning fear.*

Get Help

Who might be willing to help you rehearse your steps? It could be a parent, a therapist, a spouse or partner, or a friend. If you can't find someone to help you, be sure to at least speak your part out loud, perhaps in front of a mirror. Your lips will better remember what to do if they have said the words before.

When you rehearse, your brain gets a workout that strengthens it to do the real work. The more often you rehearse, the better you will remember. You literally form connections in your brain that will make it easier to remember what you've practiced when you're under pressure.

Remember to Breathe

You're probably going to be nervous when you begin rehearsing, even though you know it's only a practice session. Your heart may start to pound or you may feel some shortness of breath. If this happens, just remind yourself that no one can see your heart beat and it will subside when you are done. You can diminish both heart rate and respiration by changing your breathing on purpose. Use diaphragmatic breathing, cued relaxation, or your favorite other breathing method to help you remain calm (see Anxiety Busters 2 and 4). It will also help you remember to breathe when you're in the real-life situation.

For example, suppose you're practicing speaking up at a staff meeting. To make the rehearsal as real as possible, you've decided to pretend that your dining room is the meeting room. You stand outside the dining room door and:

1. Feel yourself get tense as you imagine walking into the room.
2. Use cued relaxation as you walk through the door, and again as you take a seat at the table. (This calms you.)
3. Feel yourself get tense again as you anticipate having to speak.

4. Use cued relaxation again to stay physically calm until it's time for you to speak.

5. Actually speak up, loosely following the script you planned ahead of time.

6. Use cued relaxation to calm yourself again immediately after speaking.

Now, when you go into the actual meeting, you will better remember when and how to breathe.

Rate Your Anxiety Level During Each Rehearsal

The more you practice, the less nervous you'll become. Rating your anxiety level during each rehearsal is a way of being able to really see how your anxiety decreases and to get a sense of when you're ready to begin the real thing.

Step 4: Real-Life Practice

Once you've identified your goals, developed skills, and rehearsed, it's time to get out into real life. Practicing in real life should be done in small steps that gradually increase the length of time you spend in the situation. The goal is to be able to leave the situation while still feeling calm. This is how you will unlearn your fear.

Make sure you start out with steps that have minor consequences for either success or failure. For example, if you fear driving on the highway, don't start by getting on the road during rush hour in a downpour—go on a nice day, in the middle of the afternoon, and take a stretch where the exits are close together and you can get off quickly.

Anxiety-Reduction Plan

Begin by writing an anxiety-reduction plan. This is your plan for tolerating the real-life practice session. Take a look at the sample plans here.

Anxiety-Reduction Plan: Teresa

What is my goal? *I want to go to the movies with my kids.*

Do I have the skills to do this? *Yes—I used to go to the movies before I started panicking in movie theaters. Going to the movies doesn't require anything I don't know how to do.*

My real-life practice sessions:

- *I'll start by going to a movie alone so I don't bother my kids if I blow it.*
- *I'll get to the theater a few hours ahead of the show so I*

have time to buy tickets and look around. Then I'll run some errands before coming back for the movie.

- *I'll get to the theater early so I can sit on the aisle where I can leave easily. I'll breathe and relax.*
- *I'll get up, walk out, and then return during the previews—a time when I know no one will be bothered by my practicing leaving and returning in the dark.*
- *If I get nervous, I have my reminder to breathe panic away. If I feel I need to leave to calm down, I will do that. But I will buy tickets for the next day's show before I go.*
- *I will try again the next day, and if I get nervous again, I'll go to the lobby for a while and use my breathing technique. Then I'll reenter the theater and sit down again to show myself I can.*
- *I will repeat the above experience to be sure I am confident before I take the kids.*
- *Then I'll take the kids. We'll go on a weekday when the theater will be less crowded.*

Anxiety-Reduction Plan: Kyle

What is my goal? *I want to go to happy hour on Friday with my coworkers.*

Do I have the skills to socialize? *I have practiced making small talk about work, the weather, and local sports teams. I think I'm ready.*

My real-life practice sessions:

- *Stay for 30 minutes at first. Remember to breathe. Tell myself that looking nervous isn't the end of the world.*
- *Then stay 60 minutes the next time, but without ordering food, so I won't worry about eating with them.*
- *Then I will order food, and stay until I've eaten at least some of it.*
- *After that, I will stay until the group breaks up for the evening.*

Begin the Real-Life Practice Sessions

You probably felt a little anxious just reading the title of this part of the technique! Remember: Three deep breaths and good preparation. You have a plan, you have the skills to do this, and your anxiety won't kill you.

Rate Your Anxiety Level During Each Real-Life Practice Session

It's important to rate your level of anxiety during each real-life practice session. The most difficult part of this technique is getting exactly the right degree of exposure. You want to build your competence and confidence by achieving small, gradual successes. If your anxiety goes down with each real-life practice session, you know you've achieved the right degree of exposure. If it begins to go up, you need to think about taking smaller steps.

Remember: It Won't Always Go Perfectly

What happens if you fail or get anxious while making a small step? Be grateful! This is an opportunity to evaluate what kinds of things trip you up, and to review and adjust your plan so you can get better and better. Whatever you do, don't dwell on it or tell yourself bad things about yourself. Everyone makes mistakes.

A Quick Recap

Let's go over the steps again.

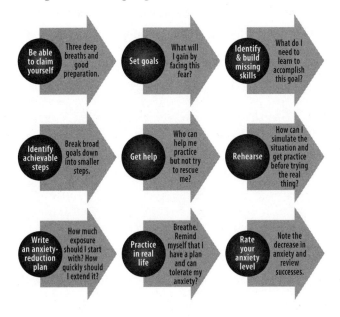

Success breeds success. Even if there are a few bumps along the way, gradually exposing yourself to the situation that scares you is how your brain unlearns fear. Every time you're able to do something without getting panicky or embarrassed, your brain says, "Hey! I thought that would be dangerous, but I guess I was wrong!" And then it's less likely to send you a "Danger!" warning in the future.

> *Success breeds success.*

Every stage of this process lays groundwork for the next step to occur safely. Once the whole goal is met, the safe experience will completely turn off the warning signal.

Because Lark's anxiety was rooted in a traumatic event, getting over her panic would be more complicated. Dr. Baum began by listening carefully to her story and asking questions about her childhood and young adult years. Her panic disorder had certainly gotten severe, but Dr. Baum was optimistic, even in spite of Lark's refusal to try medication. And just hearing his optimism made Lark feel better, too.

After several months of intensive therapy that addressed deep-seated issues like Lark's shaken confidence in her general safety, Dr. Baum asked whether she felt ready to begin gradual exposure. "We'll go slowly," he reassured her. "The whole point is to take little steps that you'll succeed at."

Lark still felt unsure, but she also desperately wanted her life back. "Okay," she said, taking a deep breath. "Where do we start?"

"Well, tell me what some of the things you miss most are. Let's start with that." Dr. Baum took out a paper and pen.

"What *don't* I miss?" Lark said. "I miss everything! But I guess if I had to pick just a few. . . . Well, part of my job is going to artists' studios—textile designers, furniture makers, that kind of thing—to find new products for the store. I don't really do that anymore, unless I know how big the studio is. But mostly I miss going out with my family, especially the annual camping trip. Just spending time with them like that, away from phones and work and. . . ." Lark gazed out the window, leaving the sentence unfinished.

"Okay, so one of your goals might be to go on the camping trip with them?"

Lark looked back at Dr. Baum. "Yes, I guess that would be a good start."

"Great. So, the next step is figuring out the skills you need to go into the situation. You've been camping before, obviously, so you already know how to do it."

Lark laughed. "Yeah, I know how to set up a tent—I just don't know how to get *in* it."

Dr. Baum smiled. "So the only skill you really need in this case is your diaphragmatic breathing, which you've been practicing for a while now. So let's talk about rehearsing the situation before you try it for real, and getting other people to help you. How could you set up a camping trial run?"

Lark thought for a moment. "Well, I guess I could set

up the tent in the living room first. I won't be as nervous if it's in the house."

"That's a great idea!" Dr. Baum seemed genuinely enthusiastic. "And you could start by getting in it for just a few minutes."

"And then I could set it up in the backyard"—Lark was on a roll—"and practice getting in it there. And if that goes well, I could try sleeping in the tent overnight."

"And maybe Celeste and James could join you?" Dr. Baum ventured.

"Yeah, Celeste would love that!" Lark jumped on the idea. "Camping in the backyard."

"It sounds like a great plan, Lark—just getting used to being in the tent in small, incremental steps. But let's go over what you'll do if you do start to feel panicky."

"Well, breathing, mostly, I guess," Lark said.

"And when are you going to do that?"

"Um, I guess I'll do it before I actually climb in, because that's when I really feel anxious. Then maybe I'll sit in the tent with the door flap open for a while, and breathe again. Then I'll zip the flap closed and breathe again. If I'm feeling like I'm going to panic, I'll open the flap back up but try to stay in the tent."

"Okay, that sounds good. And after you do the rehearsal, I want you to rate the level of anxiety you felt while you were doing it. It'll be helpful in seeing whether the exposures are working."

Over the next few weeks, Lark went through the various rehearsals. Rehearsing with the tent in the living room ended up not provoking much anxiety at all, but the backyard was a different story, especially when she zipped the flap closed. Still, Lark arrived at Dr. Baum's office afterward elated. "I did it!" she exclaimed. "It was so much fun, actually—Celeste had a blast helping me."

Dr. Baum smiled broadly. "That's terrific news. It sounds like you're ready to try the real thing."

Lark's real-life camping practice went just as well as the rehearsals. Celeste made a pillow for her that said LOVE HELPS ME HANDLE WHAT I AM GIVEN, and Lark took it with her on the outing. They chose a campsite that wasn't too far away from home, just in case she felt like she needed to abort the trip and get back to the house quickly. But no quick escapes were necessary.

The camping success was a big one, and it went a long way toward boosting Lark's confidence that she could control her panic. But there were still many more hurdles to face. Over the course of the next year, Dr. Baum helped her tackle one situation after another—and deal with the inevitable setbacks she encountered. Lark knew she was finally back on solid ground when she managed to take Celeste shopping for clothes without falling apart.

It had been a long road—one that involved everything from exploring her worst fears to taking self-defense courses at the local community college after one of the exposures had gone badly. But it had been worth it. Lark had her life back. And she was living it—really *living* it.

A Final Word

You can start really *living* your life, too. You don't have to be a prisoner to panic, social fear, or the ever-present dread of generalized anxiety. It won't be easy. But it is, actually, pretty simple. By making a conscious effort to calm your body and redirect your thoughts, you use the logical, thinking part of your brain to change the unconscious, anxious part of your brain. You teach your brain to unlearn fear and worry.

Go ahead and start now. Flip back through the book and pick one Anxiety Buster to try. Then actually *do* it. Your family will thank you. Your coworkers will thank you. And most of all, you'll thank yourself.

TIPS

10 Common Stressful Situations
and Tips on Handling Them

Flying

Traveling by air is stressful. The tickets are a big financial commitment, making it hard to change your plans, and dealing with long lines of people or missed flight connections can try anyone's patience. Plus, once you're underway, you can't stop and get off. The following tips will help you stay relaxed on the way to your destination.

Tip 1

Decide on your preferences. When do you want to board—early so you can get settled, or late so you don't have to wait onboard? Do you want to take a carry-on bag, or do you feel rushed and scrutinized trying to jam your bag in the overhead compartment while others wait? Then, stick to your plan. (Replanning your plan is just another way to worry.)

Tip 2

Prepare activities for your flight time. Music, video games, and movies are all now easy to take with you. Know how long you will be onboard and take twice as much entertainment as you'll need, including some nonelectronic choices in case batteries fail. That way you'll be set if you have to sit on the tarmac for an unexpected delay.

Tip 3

Watch your self-talk. Instead of muttering about how you hate to fly, remind yourself of how convenient it is to travel so far so fast. Don't spend time dreading the flight—instead, focus on how eager you are for the activities that lie at the end of it.

Tip 4

If you're a restless flyer, sit on the aisle—it gives you easy access to standing, stretching, and bathroom trips, which will help your muscles stay relaxed, and it's easier to avoid looking at the outside world on takeoff and landing.

Tip 5

Finally, prepare to be comfortable in every way you can think of. Wear loose clothing, in layers so you can control for temperature. For long flights, take a neck pillow. Consider investing in noise-canceling earphones (or borrow a pair). It's surprising how stressful being in such a constantly noisy environment is.

Waiting During Delays

Waiting for something that is not pleasant—whether you're at the doctor's office or stuck in traffic on the way to work—is much harder than waiting for something fun and exciting. It's easy to feel you're wasting time, and that makes the stress even more challenging.

Tip 1

Be prepared! Figure out how much time you must plan for. An hour in a doctor's waiting room? Five hours pacing in a crowded airport without a chair? Two hours in a car with no chance to stand or pace? Preparing to fill the time means you won't waste time figuring out what to do.

Tip 2

Watch your self-talk. The wait has nothing to do with you personally—no one is out to make you miserable. At the doctor's office, tell yourself that the delay means someone else is getting care she needs. At the airport, remind yourself that no airline wants delays and they really will try to get you out of there as soon as possible. When you're stuck in traffic, tell yourself that it's not a personal vendetta against you. Remind yourself that the wait will end and that you're the only one who suffers if you let yourself seethe.

Tip 3

Waiting is a good time to meditate, pray, or breathe to relax your body. You're probably not doing enough of that anyway!

Tip 4

Remember to take chargers for your electronics. Waiting seems to suck the life out of batteries, so don't get caught short on power.

Tip 5

Take whatever you need to use the time productively. Write thank-you cards, call your mother, read a journal article, knit, listen to an audio book, or actually read a book. When the amount of time you may have to wait is unpredictable, have more than one activity ready to go.

Visiting Friends or Family When Some Tensions Exist

Visiting friends or family when you don't get along perfectly can make even a celebration turn sour. Keeping your options open will make the visit less fraught with tension.

Tip 1

Remember why you're going. There's a reason—maybe a delightful one—for you to make the visit. Focus your thoughts on the good reasons to go.

Tip 2

Get your humor on. Anticipate what typically goes wrong. Whatever it is—your son-in-law drinks too much, your brother always picks a fight, your mother inevitably criticizes you— you can plan a lighthearted response or a way to make a joke to minimize the discomfort. Then stop worrying about it. You have a plan if you need it.

Tip 3

Plan break times. Get yourself ready to announce that you need some fresh air and go out for a walk—whether it's 5 minutes or 50. It could even be just a bathroom break, whether you need to use the facilities or not. Getting away for a few minutes can give you cool-down time. During the break, don't dwell on your frustration—instead, play a game on your phone, listen to some music, meditate, or just breathe.

Tip 4

If you have to stay overnight, stay in a hotel if you can afford it. If someone will be offended that you're not staying at the house, blame it on recent insomnia or allergies or just hold your ground that you think it best to have a quiet space for sleeping and breakfast. Then you can leave at night and arrive in the daytime when you are ready.

Tip 5

Have your own transportation (your own car or a rental). If you can drive yourself there, you won't have to rely on anyone else's timing. Knowing you can leave when you want to makes it easier to stay.

A Death in the Family

This is not a list on how to handle grief in five easy steps. It is intended as a quick coaching session on getting through the first stage of an important loss.

Tip 1

Attending the wake, funeral, or memorial service may be hard on you, but it's very important to everyone who cared for the person who has died. There's a saying that goes, "Sharing joy doubles the joy. Sharing grief cuts it in half." Be present. It will help you and others as well.

Tip 2

Go without judgment. Everyone grieves differently. Some wail. Some tell funny stories about their loved one. Some are numb and placidly serve coffee at a luncheon. Allow others to be as they are without weighing whether they are doing it right, and try to forgive those whose behavior may be unsuitable. Also, take in even the most banal of platitudes about loss. ("He's in a better place" takes top honors for banality.) Most people don't know what to say, but they're making an effort—be grateful that they want to comfort you. If you're not part of the immediate family, try saying something like, "I'm here to show you I care about you and your family."

Tip 3

Take it one step at a time. If you have to make decisions about the funeral, begin closing up property, or manage the finances, just do one thing at a time. Grieving while trying to do a tremendous amount of paperwork isn't easy. Don't look at the whole task—just focus on what is necessary each day.

Tip 4

Self-care at a time of grief is incredibly important. Make sure to rest even if you aren't sleeping well. Although sleep aids are not the best choice for insomnia in general, a night or two of a sleep medication might serve you well. Don't skip eating even if the food is bland or you're not hungry. When your blood sugar plummets it's harder to handle emotions. This is also a bad time to add a lot of alcohol into the mix. Blunting grief doesn't discharge it—it just delays your dealing with it. Also, it's not insensitive to get some exercise. Moving vigorously is one of the best ways to release the physical upset of stressful times. See if a family member or friend wants to join you for a walk outside. Walks can lead to a good talk and important emotional connection.

Tip 5

Make sure that someone is keeping a book for people who attend the service and is asking attendees to sign it and add comments. A family in mourning often cannot remember all the details, and a book to help them remember who came is very valuable. It's also a good place for people to share warm thoughts about the person who has died, and the family will appreciate it when the initial rush is over.

Ending Relationships With Coworkers, Romantic Partners, and Friends

Sometimes it's just time to move on. You may be moving to a new job, deciding a friendship has become stressful or is not giving much anymore, or ending a romantic relationship. Here are some tips on how to move on with grace.

Tip 1

It may seem easier to walk away without a face-to-face conversation, but in-person good-byes are a good idea for both parties involved. If you're leaving a job, see each person you worked with and tell all of them you're grateful for having the experience of working together. Even if all you learned from them was how *not* to be a colleague, you can genuinely express gratitude for the experience without describing it. If the experience was positive, by all means go into specifics. You don't have to promise to be friends for life or meet for coffee every week. Just say, "Thank you" or "I'll remember you."

Tip 2

Don't rehash previous disagreements. If you've decided a relationship is over, it's not necessary to bring up all the past conflict. Bringing up disagreements is an invitation to resolve the problems and thus continue the relationship.

Tip 3

Ending romances or friendships requires two things simultaneously: honesty and kindness. If it's genuinely over, don't offer hope, but recognize that the other person will want an explanation. "I'm just not feeling it" may be honest but it's not particularly kind. "I haven't felt the chemistry a good relationship needs, and I think it's better for us to stop seeing each other now than for me to continue under false pretenses" is as honest as "not feeling it" but much kinder. If there's a reason, give it. Do you simply not enjoy the same activities or share the same values? Just say so without suggesting that the other person is wrong not to be like you.

Tip 4

Friendships often end when one friend has become demanding and the other tires of being in the support role, or when the friendship formed over a shared activity (such as volunteer work) that one person (or both) is no longer as interested in. The significance of the relationship should direct the way you end it. A less important relationship is one you might end by attrition. Just don't accept the next invitation or two and then space out contact over greater lengths of time. If there was a serious conflict, offer an honest, kind statement that you don't want to maintain the friendship in light of the hurt. This statement can be made in writing (handwrite the note; don't e-mail) or over the phone or in person. That makes the reason clear. It's easier for the other person to get over the loss of the relationship when he or she knows why it happened.

Tip 5

Don't end a relationship by saying you might reconsider in the future. That kind of statement creates the false impression that it's not really over. It's more painful than just ending it. If you're not sure whether you'll reconsider in the future, do one of two things: Don't end the relationship now, or end it cleanly now and contact the person again to ask for a fresh start after you've reconsidered.

Saying No

For some people, saying no feels equivalent to insulting some-one. But being able to say no is necessary if you want to con-serve some of your own time and energy.

Tip 1

Make a rule that from now on, no matter what anyone asks of you, you will say: "Give me a minute to check my schedule" or "Let me get back to you—I need to check if I can do that." Say this for every single request. Then take the time to actually decide if the request is something you want to do or have time to do.

Tip 2

If you're undecided about whether you should do it, do a quick cost-benefit analysis. How much will it cost you to say yes, and how much will it benefit you? Don't ask how much it will help the person who's asking! If you can see that it will cost you too much time, effort, money, and so on, it'll be easier for you to say no.

Tip 3

In work situations, watch your self-talk. Don't tell yourself you're indispensable (you're not) and don't assume that your extra work is what's keeping the company afloat. If there's a good reason to take someone's shift or stay late to finish a job, consider a negotiation to get the time back later, or get a trade. ("If I do this, can you do that?") Remember, people are asking for your help because they want to make their lives easier. It's up to you to protect your own time.

Tip 4

If you're saying no at home to children, remember this: It's good for children to learn to deal with frustration. The world isn't going to give them everything they ask for, and your "no" prepares them to handle that. If you're dealing with other family members, say no when you would be inconvenienced in terms of time, money, or emotional stamina.

Tip 5

You may say yes to make other people happy with you. Two points here. First, if you have to give someone else everything he asks for to make him happy, it's unlikely that you'll ever really be able to make him happy. So don't try. Second, you can't ever know if saying no actually will make the person unhappy. He may have come to you first but easily be able to go to someone else, do it himself, or live without what he asked for. Regardless, it's not your job to make everyone else happy—especially not at your own expense.

Meeting New People

Whether you're going to a party, starting at a new school, going to a conference, entering into a business networking group, volunteering at an event, or meeting other parents at a school function, you might feel nervous about whether you'll be able to talk to others, be accepted, and pull it all off without embarrassment. Here are a few tips to increase your comfort level.

Tip 1

Have a visual image of where you'll be. It helps to be able to see the site or the type of gathering in your mind ahead of time. If you don't know the conference center or restaurant, you can probably look it up online. It's easier to see yourself doing well in the setting if you know what it will look like.

Tip 2

Know the situation. Call the event coordinator and ask a few questions: How many people are likely to attend? Will there be a social time before the meeting or meal? Will attendees have name tags? If you're starting at a new school or college, ask whether someone can show you around before classes get underway. You may be able to meet professors or teachers ahead of time too, just to say hello.

Tip 3

Watch for negative self-talk. Interrupt your inner voice when it tells you that you aren't as smart or interesting as everyone else, or when it berates you for saying something "dumb." Instead, focus on how you can pay attention to others. Remember, you're not the only shy person there—others want to be accepted by you as much as you want to be accepted by them.

Tip 4

Smile and say hello with a brief eye contact. If you hate eye contact, you can look at the space right between the eyes at the top of the nose and people will think you have looked them in the eye. In a group that is milling about, go stand with people who are already chatting, say "hi," and then listen. You may think of something to add, or someone may ask you a question to include you.

Tip 5

Remember the adage "It's easier to be interested than to be interesting." Think ahead of time about appropriate questions you can ask people at the function. For example, at a meeting for parents of kids in the school band, you can ask other parents about their children, whether the parents also play instruments, how long they've lived in the area, and so on. At a wedding, ask other guests how they know the bride or groom. At a business meeting your questions can be about the company or the product line.

Interviews

Job or college interviews come with their special level of stress because there is a lot at stake. You know making a good impression is important. Practicing ahead of time is always smart—it boosts your confidence, which helps you do your best in a situation where you're going to be judged.

Tip 1

Do your homework. For any interview, knowing about the company or school—its history, products, mission statement, and so on—will make it easier for you to ask questions or make relevant comments.

Tip 2

Never say anything bad or self-deprecating about yourself, even as a joke. When the interviewer asks about your weaknesses or flaws, focus on what you've learned from a past experience. Practice this ahead of time.

Tip 3

Be confident. Enter the interview ready to shake a hand and smile with eye contact. Bring a written list of questions (about job expectations, training that will be offered, supervision, etc.) and don't be afraid to refer to it. Having a written list shows that you're prepared and communicates your interest in doing well. When asked about your skills, be ready to say what they are without exaggerating.

Tip 4

Stating your own expectations is part of any interview. For a job interview, research the average salaries for the position and ask for the high end of that range. Women tend to understate their competence and ask for less, expecting to be offered what they deserve instead. I once had a client, a business owner, who told me he paid three different employees different salaries for doing the same work—all because he'd been able to negotiate lower salaries for some of them. At a school, you may be asked about why you want to attend that specific school. State what you hope you to do with your degree, as well as any needs you have if you're applying for a scholarship.

Tip 5

Ending the interview with a good handshake really matters, so practice yours. (Seriously!) If it's weak, floppy, or stiff, loosen your fingers, meet the other's palm, and grasp warmly but briefly. Remember to ask what time frame they have for making a decision. Also, prepare and practice an exit line—something along the lines of, "Thanks for this opportunity. I look forward to hearing from you." This will increase your chances that you will hear from them.

Taking Tests

Taking a test without anxiety involves being prepared and managing your attitude.

Tip 1

Prepare! Without preparation you can't face the test calmly. Ask questions ahead of time about what kind of test it is so that you can correctly visualize the process. Is it multiple choice or essay? Typed or handwritten? If there are study questions or practice tests available, use them.

Tip 2

You've heard it a million times, but do get enough rest the night before. You'll actually remember more if you sleep 8 hours than if you sleep less. Also, eat something before the test. Your brain uses about 20% of your calories each day—don't deprive it of energy if you want it to perform!

Tip 3

Arrive in the classroom a few minutes early and take that time to breathe deeply, stretch your muscles, clear your mind, and invite "everything I already know about this material to be available to me while I take this test."

Tip 4

Look over the entire test quickly before you begin it. Knowing what's coming will reduce your anxiety and help you better gauge your time. Also, if there are certain things you're trying to remember, write them down (in keywords) in the margin as soon as the test is handed out. That way you don't have to worry about forgetting them partway through.

Tip 5

Watch out for negative self-talk. Berating yourself about not knowing an answer or comparing yourself unfavorably to students who are finishing faster won't help you remember the material better or answer any faster. Instead, remind yourself that you prepared to the best of your ability. You can also boost your confidence by answering the easiest questions first and going back to the harder ones toward the end. If you're afraid of failing, remind yourself that failing a test is not the same as failing life! You'll have chances in the future to do better.

Vacations

Vacations are supposed to be relaxing, but if you haven't packed what you need—or if you have trouble leaving work behind or worry about not being at home—they can end up being stressful.

Tip 1

Preparation is key to packing well. Start writing down a list of what you need to take before you start packing. List the activities you'll do while away and write down what you will wear for each. List all necessary toiletries and games or books. Write down what goes into your smaller bag. Identification and money are the two essentials to remember. Take flight and hotel confirmation numbers in writing as well as in your electronic device. If you're traveling abroad, make sure passports are ordered in plenty of time, and check on whether you need a visa. For all travel, photocopy all of your documents and your credit cards, front and back, and carry them in a separate place, not in your wallet or purse.

Tip 2

If you're a fussy eater or have children of any age with you, be sure to take snacks that don't crush and don't need refrigeration. Low blood sugar can make you irritable, and it may not be convenient to stop and buy food.

Tip 3

Plan your first day away to be more relaxing than hectic. This gives you a day to unwind before heading into high-activity mode. Also, consider coming home a day before you have to return to work. You'll feel less compelled to check in on work during vacation if you know you have a day to catch up before heading to the office, and it also gives you time to unpack, do the laundry, get some groceries, and so on.

Tip 4

If you have trouble leaving work behind, figure out why. Is it just a feeling of compulsion? (Push it aside and distract yourself from checking e-mail or making calls.) Do you worry that you'll lose your job if people don't see you there? Afraid that important issues won't be taken care of? Once you know what compels you to check in, make a plan. Discuss with coworkers how to handle things in your absence. Discuss with your boss how to handle that important project when you're not there to answer a question. Make arrangements for emergency contact, not regular checking in, if you fear decisions cannot be made without you. If you still can't bear to separate from work, then designate one hour a day as work time, preferably in the morning. Then be done for the rest of the day so that you can be present with your family or traveling companions.

Tip 5

If you worry about bad things happening at home while you're away, make a list of what needs to be done (close windows, leave instructions for house sitter, etc.) before you leave, and check off the items. If you find worries continuing to crop up, ask yourself what is possible versus probable. If it's only possible, just let the thought go and distract yourself. If it's probable, make a plan. Is the weather forecast calling for thunderstorms that might knock out power to the sump pump? Ask a neighbor to check in and make sure she has your emergency contact information. Still worrying? Ask yourself, "What's the worst that could happen?" Remind yourself that you can handle even the worst outcome.

INDEX

Index